I COVER THE WATERFRONT

I COVER THE WATERFRONT ~

STORIES FROM THE SAN DIEGO SHORE

By
MAX MILLER

Skyhorse Publishing

First Skyhorse Publishing edition 2014

10 9 8 7 6 5 4 3 2 1

Library of Congress Cataloging-in-Publication Data is available on file.

Cover design by Owen Corrigan

Print ISBN: 978-1-62914-454-2
Ebook ISBN: 978-1-63220-002-0

Printed in the United States of America

I COVER THE WATERFRONT

I

I HAVE been here so long that even the sea gulls must recognize me. They must pass the word along about me from generation to generation, from egg to egg.

Former friends of mine, members of my old university class, acquaintances my own age, have gone out to earn their six thousand a year. They have become managers, they have become editors, they have become artists. Yet here am I, what I was six years ago, a waterfront reporter.

True, I am called a good waterfront reporter in this city, as if the humiliation were not already great enough in itself. I shudder at the compliment, yet should feel fortunate in a way that so far I have escaped the word veteran. When I am called not only the best waterfront reporter but also the veteran waterfront reporter, then for sure all hope is dissolved. And I need look ahead then, only to that day when the company presents me with a fountain pen and a final check.

I am nearing twenty-eight, and should I by accident be invited to a home where literature is discussed, or styles, or Europe, the best I could do would be to crawl into the backyard. There I could sit tossing pebbles into the fountain until the hostess found me out. If she compelled me to come back into the house and join the conversation, my topics would have to be of swordfishing, or of lobstering, or of hunting sardines in the dark of the moon, or of fleet gunnery practice, or of cotton shipments. The predicament has passed beyond my control. I am one of those creatures who remain permanent, who stay in one place, that successful men on returning home may see for the happiness of comparison. I am of the damned and the lost, and yet I do know more than I did six years ago when I first came here, a graduate in liberal arts.

I existed my first season on this waterfront buoyed by that common hope of mankind that by next year I would write a book, a novel composed of the characters I met. Quite tidily, too, I would insert my own silent sufferings, such as eating at the lunch counter downstairs where the sugar bowl is always chucked with brown lumps. These fishermen will dip coffee spoons back into it for the third or fourth helping. But instead of writing of this, I learned instead to take the lazy man's course and drink my coffee without sugar.

The second year blended into the third. The characters I had picked out for my novel gradually became more blurred to my complete understanding. Nobody was definitely good, nobody was definitely bad. The more I knew of them the less positive I became of which stand to take, and for a novel a writer does need a villain; a writer needs several of them. Even Evangeline, the brown-haired waitress, proved a disappointment to my plans. I had selected her to be the waterfront harlot. I had a drab death already prescribed for her, a death in which she would fling herself from the tugboat pier with only the silver moon as witness. The gentle bosom of the bay would cleanse her of her sorrow, would baptise her anew, and she would be carried by the tide to sea with a look of peace upon her world-wronged face. But unfortunately Evangeline does not need cleansing. In fact she has a home and a husband, rather a nice chap. He is a quartermaster on a destroyer based here. And even now I can hardly forgive Evangeline for this trick on me.

Of course if a writer were really desperate for harlots there are plenty of them around here. They follow the fleet from port to port as regularly as the wake of the vessels, but a person has to be an expert to distinguish them. I see the girls come down to the float where the shoreboats land, but often enough they turn out to be dutiful wives or high-school daughters. And the sailors, especially, are wise enough to keep their mouths shut until they know for sure.

At any rate the original characters I selected for my book never did show up. I have yet to see them. I do not know what has happened to them, but I have waited six years. I can wait no longer; I am getting too old, so must go ahead with what I already have on hand.

My studio, by the way, is upstairs in the tugboat office. The room is not mine. It belongs to the publicity agent of the deep-sea fishing barge. Until this book he has been a critic of all I write. When my news stories concerned his fishing barge he clipped them out. He keeps a scrapbook to show his employer at the end of the season. Some of my writings are being saved. I under-estimated myself.

The walls of this room are decorated with pictures of bluefin, yellowfin, skipjack, barracuda and mackerel. These are my inspiration. They are the left-over pictures he could not peddle to the papers. Men are holding the fish. The pictures where women are holding the fish are peddled. They were printed. He has none of them left but he keeps the others here.

The shingles of the roof show through the ceiling. The roof slopes so low on the south side that a person cannot stand up there. The room is quite small, and in summer stuffy with a sort of cobweb stuffiness.

Frequently the tugboat operators come up to see the publicity agent, my lone encouragement. They have questions to be answered, yet mostly they desire to read his library. The book in it is Rabelais, illustrated. He keeps it locked in the middle drawer to the right. The operators must not take the book downstairs to the pier, but must read it in the room, and first must see that their hands are wiped of grease. He keeps an eye secretly on them as they read; he is deathly afraid that one of them with a pencil might some day add insulting shadows to the naked ladies. And all this, then, is the ultimate of my literary environment. I who would have consented six years ago to have done book reviews while waiting for the job of theatre critic.

The two windows, small and unmovable, furnish a clear sweep of the harbor through their film of dirt. The sea gulls come and perch near the window ledges. The birds stare in at me and I stare out at them. During these interviews we both carry rather silly expressions, for neither of us seems to know what he is going to do next. They act as if they, too, have read up on the universe around us and are wise to the fact that in this jumble of orbits we are foolish to have ambitions, that we are foolish to do anything all day long except eat. In a million million years the whole show will be ended anyhow, and so why should they or I acquire wrinkles trying to amount to something. Whereupon, we merely stand and stare, passengers on the same boat.

The pelicans now are different, specially the old pelicans which perch on the pier-heads beyond the windows. The pelicans have worried so much about life that the tops of their heads are gray. They have worried and worried, yet have arrived nowhere either. They do not even bother to look in the window at me. Each day has become as much a burden to them as their heavy bills. They are tired, so tired they have forgotten how to make a noise. They are so tired they no longer can be bothered scrambling for food.

At first they must have despised the sea gulls for all of their squawking and for all of their swooping for scraps and for their greedy habit of robbing the nests of the cormorants. They must have regarded sea gulls much as I regard committee people, and yet the pelicans in time must have grown up, which is more than I can do. They must have forced themselves to consider the sea gull in its better moments, when its stomach is stuffed to the limit, when it is content to sit by these windows staring in at me as though it too is filled with reasoning. All sea

gulls, I think, would ultimately like to be pelicans, but so far are too earthy to overcome their
appetites.

And so I do have my acquaintances, after all,
in my studio upstairs on the tugboat pier.

II

EACH year we go after elephant seals for the Zoo. Sometimes we go in the navy's tugboat, *Koka,* sometimes in the Navy's Eagle boat 34. We cruise to that Mexican island of Guadalupe.

There on the sands the monsters are awaiting us. They comprise the only herd of their kind in existence, and they are too contented with themselves to be angry at our intrusion.

They have basked in the sunlight of those islands for hundreds of years now, and who are we? We are a pestilence of germs to carry them away. Only they do not recognize germs. They fear nothing they cannot recognize.

From the vessel we float the sides of a cage ashore through the surf. The frames are covered with paddock-fencing of the strongest. On the beach we put the cage together, leaving the shore-end open.

We walk through the herd selecting the member we want, although all look healthy enough. Their black eyes are as doorknobs, their sea-washed hides catch the Mexican sun and radiate it back at us. Their long noses are like sawed-off elephant trunks, and they turn these noses up at us as we walk past. We do not belong here. They can tell this by sniffing.

We select the one we wish, not because of his size, but because of his convenience to the cage. We shoo him backwards into the cage. We threaten to hit him in the snout if he does not back up, yet he weighs a ton and a half; he weighs as much as all of us twice over.

When he is in the cage, and the cage is secure, we wait for the tide to rise; then we float the cage out to the vessel. The ship's crane hoists the load aboard, and the ship's pumps are turned upon the captive to keep him wet. If he is not kept wet he moves about scratching himself and fretting.

Sometimes we bring back three at a time. We can bring back as many as we have room for, as the herd must number half a thousand. Sometimes we see them swimming far offshore long before we reach the island. They are so big that you imagine you are looking at some sea-monster these many years extinct.

But fifty years ago there used to be lots of elephant seals around here, old fishermen say. The elephant seals used to come as far north as Southern California. Everybody thought the herd had all been killed off until these were found at Guadalupe. The Mexican Government does not permit them to be killed now, and the expedition has to get permission from Mexico City before making the capture. This always takes a long time.

The only syndicate stories I am ever sure of selling are about elephant seals. Nobody seems to be anxious to buy my short stories or my opinions, but I can always market copy on elephant seals. They are my lone entrée into literature. Nor are my words sufficient in themselves. My stories must be illustrated. This fact used to humiliate me four or five years ago, but now I am hardened, and I am grateful for any outside check.

For other reasons, too, I consider myself quite an elephant-seal expert; I am the elephant-seal editor. I know that the only time the bulls are the least bit vicious is during May and June. This is mating season for them, and as each bull is fond of collecting a harem the fighting among the bulls is terrific. They bunt each other against the sharp rocks of Guadalupe until one or the other gives up and dies. They do not bite. Their mouths are not built for biting. They simply slam each other without mercy; then for the remaining ten months are on the best of terms with all the world. To bear their calves the cows go away into hiding on the opposite side of the island. Some caves are there and cows like to be around caves.

On these expeditions I like to pretend that I

am far away on the other side of the earth and
am really doing something for science. The
desolate island with its bleak cliffs helps me play
the secret little game. But the game is always
short-lived, for in actuality we are only a night
and a day away from the city, and we are back in
port before we know it. Even our captures are
no surprise to the city, for the success of the expedition had been radioed on ahead to the Zoo.
Trucks and a crane are on the pier to meet us.
The trucks parade the giants through the streets
to the Zoo tank, and always the creatures are so
large that their tails drag along the cement, and
persons stare.

The Zoo officials thank us in such a way that I
always leave the grounds feeling a little silly.
The officials know there is no danger connected
with the capture, but I wish they didn't.

III

EACH two weeks a liner from New York arrives, and we three waterfront reporters go out in a shoreboat to meet her before she docks.

We are three agents of Heaven sent out ahead to inspect the latest shipload of souls before they land.

But of course our inspection is only secondhand, as the passengers have been graded and labeled before they left New York.

Their names have been sent overland by the line's publicity service, but we must make sure they are still aboard, that they did not get off at Panama, and besides, our papers want pictures of them.

I used to feel mortified at the task of meeting liners, but now I do not mind. I used to believe what I read in books about all passengers considering ships' reporters a nuisance, but now I do not know for sure. Or perhaps habit has deadened my nerves. As a reporter I may have become what I most feared I would become, "typical."

Outside the channel we board the liner as soon

as the quarantine flag goes down. We climb a
Jacob's ladder, a camera-man with us, to the first
hatch.

The passengers bend over the starboard rail-
ings to watch us. The three of us, or sometimes
there are only two of us, are that "flock" of reporters which famous beings are always en-
countering in novels. We are the "flock" of reporters from whom famed beings are always
hiding. When novelists get real mean they have
us entering rooms with our hats on, and they
have us diving for the sandwich plate with both
hands and a pocket. And they have us persisting
with our questions until finally the hero hauls off
and knocks us out.

We, then, are these reporters. We swing
aboard, and the line's publicity agent swings
aboard with us. The ship's purser says hello to
us, and he calls us by name, and he tells us which
stateroom belongs to us. Sometimes when he is
not too busy he comes with us to the stateroom,
bringing a passenger list with him. He rings for
a steward who brings into the stateroom refresh-
ments taken aboard during the vessel's stop at
Havana. The steward also brings three bottles
of soda water.

"Not much," we say, "because we're working."
Or sometimes if the liner has arrived too late for
the day's edition, we do not say this. He tells us

who is aboard who would make copy. If we have our doubts, the line's publicity agent goes on deck and finds out. The camera-man goes with him, and we three reporters stay and talk with the purser, and sometimes the chief engineer comes in and talks too. The chief engineer on one of the liners always wants to know if we can get him tickets to the fights held in the city each Friday night. Sometimes we can, and so we sit there talking and sipping the fumes from Havana, and the purser and the engineer tell us about the women aboard. This always seems their duty, to take care of the women aboard who travel alone and after the first week get lonely. The purser and the engineer like to tell us about them. And after awhile the line's publicity agent comes back into the stateroom.

"Well, I got a few items," he will say. "But a deader ship I've never seen. It's terrible."

He pours himself a bit, then recites the items and names to us and we copy them on our copy paper. Or sometimes the office has told us to get a special story on a special passenger. Then we talk with him ourselves, and the bigger he is the easier he is to talk with. And often we find that we, and not the passenger, are the ones being interviewed. They ask us as many questions as we ask them, and sometimes they like to come along with us back to the stateroom for a bit of the bottle, and to talk with us there about the city they are entering. The liner continues sliding through the channel toward the pier. This always takes at least an hour as the gangway is a slow thing to handle even after the lines are on the dock.

If I were given all New York to cover for a week I doubt if I could run into as many honest conversations with as many honest big men as I have experienced in this little bay of sunlight. The days on the ocean coming up from Panama have rested their minds, I believe, and they are not so eager to be distrustful of all human faces. They tell us any number of secrets which we know they do not want printed, and so we do not print them. Nor do years blur the memory of these conversations.

I can recall as if yesterday the half-cloudy morning Jack Dempsey told us he came to town to get married, and would we hold off the story until he bought the license. We went with him, and he introduced us reporters to Miss Taylor. Not one of us had the heart to violate such courtesy, but to the contrary we felt as if we were confederates with him in the plot for secrecy.

I remember the uncomfortably hot morning— and it must have been years and years ago— that Charlie Chaplin arrived on the *Emma Alexander* to film the fade-out scene of "The Gold

Rush." His cast was ordered to be ready for work at sunrise. The members were ready for work at sunrise, each weighed beneath Alaskan furs. They were still ready at nine and they were still ready at eleven, each face a spectacle of discomfort as the sun struck at them. Chaplin had gone ashore somewhere, and at noon he appeared, walking up the pier with one foot in a gunnysack. Very well, he should apologize, should he, and he the man who was paying them.

I remember going out into the harbor to interview Laura LaPlante, waiting on shipboard for the filming of "The Midnight Sun." She stood by the railing in all her make-up and sniffling most frightfully. She had a wretched cold but dare not use a handkerchief because her face would have to be re-made. I cannot look at one of her pictures now without remembering the hopelessness of this tragedy.

Nor how could I ever regret the months donated to Charles Lindbergh. "Slim," we called him. And all this was before he was yanked away from the earth-dwellers and sanctified into membership with the Deity. All this was while he was hanging around here waiting for his monoplane to be completed. All this was while the desk still considered him just another goof out to get publicity. He would thank me each time I succeeded getting in a story on him. I think he wanted the clippings to send to his backers in St. Louis. He wanted to show them he was not sleeping.

His hat sat so stiffly on his head that sometimes it was embarrassing to walk into a restaurant with him. He was so gawky then; he was as a farmer boy still in the torturous throes of growth. Somebody later must have whispered to him about his hat, perhaps Ambassador Herrick. For it was changed immediately after his ascent into sainthood. We who know him around the small plane factory felt it our duty to look out after him. There was so much about life he apparently did not know. We guided him about as we would a high-school child on his first trip to the city. A tribe of beings have this God-given gift of seeming helplessness, and he was a member of the tribe. Of course, it was obvious to all of us that he knew planes almost to the point of fanaticism. Otherwise we would have had nothing to do with him. The editors, not being on the field or in the factory, had no way of seeing this fanatical knowledge of his at work, and so it is no wonder they doubted our copy about him. He was honest with a strange, big-eyed honesty, but even we, his friends, doubted if he would get across. He was too innocent to get anywhere.

"Slim, you ought to go on an exciting party."

There were four of us in my room when this

suggestion was made to him. We had come to
my room after lunch for a smack of cognac. A
French vessel had just been in port, and I had
boarded her. We were sitting around, the four
of us, Frank Mahoney, who owned the factory,
and "Adolph" Edwards, the factory's chief sales-
man and its only one. We had long ago stopped
offering a glass to "Slim," as his answer was
always the same. It was simply a waste of time,
and besides we did feel like his protectorates; we
felt as though we were all his trainers and that
he was the only member of the football team.
Each of us had to look out after him.

"But, Slim, you ought to go on at least one
party," Edwards repeated.

"I'd like to," he confessed. "Honest, I'd like
to." His tone had such a wistfulness about it,
such a helpless desire to study the mechanics of
sin, that the three of us felt like conspirators of
the blackest.

"I know . . ." Frank Mahoney saved the day.
"I know, Slim. You just wait till you get to
Paris. They have all kinds of parties there."

"I'll be broke, though."

Frank thought a moment: "You can sell your
plane."

"I figured on that, but it will be just enough
money to get me back. The thing will have had
so many hours."

To be sure, this was a problem.

Yet today, here I am, performing in a way I had vowed never to perform, writing reminiscences of Slim.   Or at least one reminiscence. Yet perhaps I may be forgiven as the original point in mind was not to write of him, but to show how even reporters way out here, even waterfront reporters, frequently enough have experiences handed them in a bucket—experiences for which New York reporters would have waited in an ante-room.

Or again, there are statesmen and politicians. But everybody sooner or later gets to talk with them.   Herbert Hoover, before he was nominated, slipped into town by train one morning. With his overcoat under his arm he hurried, almost ran, from the station to the waterfront, my waterfront.

I was playing the slot machine in front of the pier's cigar store, and when I looked up there was Herbert Hoover.   Nobody as far as I know had expected him.   But there he stood.   Of course, it was now up to me to get to work.   Yet, strangely enough, I did not feel a bit excited in a reportorial way.

"Hello," I said, my hand still poised on the slot-machine lever.   "What are you doing around here?"

For all I know I may have continued pulling down the lever.   My nickel was in the machine, but I do not remember watching the fruit spin around, nor do I recall taking any chips from the cup.

Also I must have informed him I was from a newspaper, because he answered my question. He said he was waiting to go out on the *Albacore* for a fishing trip off Lower California. The *Albacore* is operated by the fish and game commission. He said he had not made up his mind to go until this morning. He thought he would have good weather for the trip, now that the wind had changed back to the northwest.

I thought so too. We gossiped on. Finally the little *Albacore* sped with a flourish alongside the boat landing. He boarded her, and departed.

And again, there was Gertrude Ederle, then a big name. She was on a theatre run. For a feature story I swam with her across the bay channel. When I was still only three-fourths across, she had reached the opposite shore. She whispered an apology for having swum so fast, "But I couldn't help it, the water's so cold."

And there was Babe Ruth. Also on a theatre tour. He wanted to catch a jewfish. I got a boat free for him from the tugboat company. We caught no jewfish. We caught five mackerel. The skipper brought along a bunch of new baseballs. On the way back to port, Ruth autographed them, asking each of us how we spelled our names. I was so secretly proud of my ball that in repentance as much as anything I mailed it to my young nephew.

But I have started a chapter I cannot finish; I have started a chapter I am not entitled to finish. For it is absurd to imagine I know these magical beings. They are but shadows to me, shadows which arrive and disappear, shadows which would mean utterly nothing to me except for the aura of publicity given them elsewhere by others. Hoover would have been an oddly dressed man coming to the waterfront on a day off from his hardware store. Miss Ederle would have been a country cousin whom I took swimming on one of "my off-swimming days." Slim would have been an adolescent youngster with a bent for mechanics. And Ruth—a big-hearted bruiser whose humor was of a logging-camp crudity.

This week another liner will arrive. I shall board her and meet more shadows. In another two weeks another liner will arrive, and again I shall board her, and again I shall meet more shadows. Some of the shadows will impress me as "interesting" on their own; in others I shall have to interpret "interest," having been warned it is there. But this I do know; we reporters, like the lost children of the wilderness, build our own gods. Then we stand around in awe of them. We feel grateful when they nod at us. And yet they are made from the tappings of our own typewriters. I wish a liner some day would bring a man into the harbor who would take me aside and in a fatherly way explain it all to me.

IV

A PORTUGUESE tuna-clipper returned to port today after riding out a chabasco storm off the Mexican coast. Although nobody had been lost I went aboard the clipper anyway. The crew was still rather scared, as these chabascos are bad medicine, being a mixture between a cyclone and a typhoon.

The sea had torn around the decks plenty, all right. The tuna in the hold had to be thrown over the side because the refrigeration had broken down during the blow. The chipped ice in the storage had all melted, and the men were disgusted about the whole thing.

They had been to sea twenty-eight days and had run into a fair catch around Clipperton island. They were on their way home when the chabasco caught them. It was bad, but not bad enough for a real news story. For storms at sea do not mean much to readers unless a fisherman or two is washed overboard, or unless the clipper is driven ashore.

These tuna they catch down south are big fellows, weighing up into the hundreds of pounds. Three men work together in hoisting each fish aboard. They have to work fast, for the school is all around them and biting as rapidly as the hooks drop back into the water. The proper name for what they use is not hooks, at least not regular fishhooks as used by sportsmen.

These fishermen on tuna-clippers do not have barbs on their hooks, nor for that matter bait either. They use the feathers off rooster necks instead. These feathers are long and in the water they resemble live squids. The tuna, if they are biting at all, dive after these imitation squids and are caught by the hooks.

The fishermen are too clever to waste any time. As soon as a tuna strikes for the feathers the three fishermen working in a team hoist their line aboard. In this way the tuna is sent sailing through the air by the momentum of its own strike. The idea works beautifully. Nevertheless, a lot of work is connected with catching a hundred tons.

Because the hooks have no barbs, the fishermen do not have to stop to take off each fish they catch. Rather, the fish is thrown off on its own accord upon the deck, and later is dropped down into the hatch with the chipped ice. But with so many fishing teams working at once with a school, the hooks are flying everywhere and some of the men become badly cut up. They sometimes have their eyes put out, and now many of the men wear heavy masks of wire over their faces. The masks are re-made from those used by baseball players.

A friend of mine once was knocked out by a flying squid. He was a young fellow, an Italian. He was the chummer. This meant he had to stand on the edge of the bait tank and throw out live sardines to start the tuna biting. Once the tuna start biting, nothing will stop them. They will go after colored cloth or anything. But to get them started all clippers carry sardines in a bait tank of running water. This young Italian who was struck in the forehead by a squid was transferred unconscious to a liner bound towards Panama. He was cared for by the ship's doctor, but is back in town now with a white scar directly over his nose. He refuses to put to sea again on a clipper, and so works as a fish cleaner in one of the markets.

Yet flying squids are not feared by the fishermen as much as a chabasco. For they also strike without notice and they throw their seas just every which way. The men run below and stay there, pulling the hatches shut after them. On this Portuguese tuna-clipper the skipper alone remained in the pilot house. He stuck there at the wheel. Navigation was out of the question. All he could do was try to hold his vessel from being swamped in a trough.

He stayed in the pilot house alone for **two**

days and two nights, and still the storm showed
no signs of let-up. Nobody could come from the
forecastle to relieve him, and he wanted very
much to pray. He thought a whole lot about
wanting to pray, but the chapel on a Portuguese
clipper is well aft of the pilot house and has to
be reached from the open deck.

His clipper represented an investment of
ninety thousand dollars and he did not want to
lose it, for much of the money was his own. He
did not think of his own life, he said, but he
thought only of the clipper. He was hungry and
thirsty and so tired he hardly could see what he
was doing. The spray drove against the pilot-
house windows as though driven by a hose, and
when daylight came the storm was as high as
ever. He could not stand it any more.

He squeezed his way through the starboard
door and he grasped his way aft toward the
chapel. When the seas came at him he clung to
whatever he could find. He reached the lee of
the chapel door and entered. But the holy vestments were not inside, nor the holy coronet.
Nothing was there except the bare room, tiny
and cold and wet. He remembered, then, that
the wife of one of the fisherman had taken all
the holy gear to her home to clean them of their
sea-tarnish. The clipper had left port ahead of
time, and in the haste of departure the vestments

had been forgotten. He knew for sure, now, why the chabasco was out to get him, and that he must do something right away.

He tried to call to the men in the forecastle. He wanted to know if any of them had a prayer book or a cross he could worship. But the men, of course, could not hear him. A high sea came at him over the bow, and to dodge the sea he plunged into the slicker locker. He saw an old calendar picture on the wall there, and he tore it free from its four tacks.

The picture was of a great man, he said, a very great man. "I carry him back to the chapel. I pray to him." The skipper intimated that when a man at sea is in a bad way for something to worship he cannot be too particular. He must grab at straws and that usually the first straw will be the miracle. He did not know this then, he said, but he knows it now. He told me to remember his experience for my own good should I ever be in a similar fix. For the chabasco disappeared—in about five hours.

I asked him the name of the picture, and he answered that the picture was still on the altar in the chapel. He asked me not to print a word of it in the paper for fear he might be called a "no speak truth fellow."

"Hardly that," I assured him. "But just the same I'll not mention it in the paper."

The promise was easy to keep. I walked aft to the chapel and saw the picture he had torn out and placed there—the picture, incidentally, being an ancient one of Al Smith.

V

HE is a cripple, and he moves about the waterfront on a contraption of three wheels. They are too low to be off a bicycle, and the framework is like a skeleton, a skeleton of a vehicle long dead.

The way I happen to know how he makes his living is because I was downstairs in the tug-boat office when he wheeled himself to the doorway.

"Hello," Clarke Andrews said to him.

"Hello," the cripple answered. "I brought these new ones you wanted to see."

"Let's see them, then. Hey, you fellows, come see them. They're good."

The cripple brought out a booklet from inside his shirt. He began turning the pages. The characters were plagiarisms from comic strips. The characters were all drawings of comic-strip people undressed.

"How much?" Clarke Andrews asked.

"A dollar'n half."

"Pretty much but keep on turning."

"If I keep on turning you'll not want to buy it. They get better later on."

"Keep on turning. We'll buy it all right, won't we, fellows? We'll buy it all right."

"You said you'd buy the photographs and you didn't."

"But you asked too damned much for them. Besides they weren't much good. They were blurred."

"But you said you'd buy them and you didn't. You looked at them but you didn't buy them."

"We'll buy this all right. These are good. These are rich. Keep on turning."

The cripple turned the pages. He turned them slowly, so the men could read the words in the balloons. Perhaps this was the way the cripple had of getting back at men who were not cripples, perhaps this was the way he had of laughing at them by showing them pictures of themselves. Or perhaps again he simply wanted to make a living in the only way he knew. I don't know. I cannot even guess. All I can say is that when he got through showing the booklet he turned to Andrews and held it out for him to take.

But Andrews didn't take it. He said, "Hell, that ain't got half the kick in it you said it had. Hell, a guy can get pictures almost as good as that right in them magazines. Hell."

The cripple bit his lips but said nothing. Besides, the law, too, was against him. He backed his contraption from the doorway. He swung the wheels around and started to go.

"Here, I'll buy it," Olaf Smith said. Olaf is one of the shoreboat operators. He works for Andrews. "Here's the dollar'n half."

The cripple held out the booklet and Olaf took it. The cripple wheeled away then, leaving Olaf standing there with the naked purchase in his hand.

Olaf came back to Andrews and handed the booklet to him. "Here, Andrews. Take it home and show it to your kids. I've always wanted to give you a present, anyway. You've got it coming. You're such a swell fellow."

VI

OUR harbor here has Chris Loch. We do not boast of him, but he is here, and for a living he drags the bay with hooks. He sells whatever he finds which can be sold.

A salvager, perhaps, is the technical title for him. Yet the title somehow does not fit. He is a deep-chested man, such as is shown in the illustrations for sailing-vessel stories. But I do not know if he ever has been on a sailing vessel, I never have asked him.

His beard is cement gray, coming to a brusque point, the beard of a duelist. He must have respect for the health of his hair for he keeps it brushed, though not parted. Yes, I am sure it is not parted, although it does wave heavily to port as if blown there by the wind.

He works bareheaded. A hat makes him feel cramped, he says, and grouchy and indoors.

He was one of the first of the waterfront veterans I saw on arriving at the waterfront. There is a character, I thought, who will make a feature story some day. I must keep him in mind. I kept him in mind. This was six years ago.

This was six years ago, to repeat. And if at

that time some angel, like some sea gull, had
fluttered on to the pier and told me that in six
years I would still be here, still going the rounds
of this sunny little world, I would have been surprised—as surprised as if some angel today
would prophesy the same for the end of the six
years next to come.

Chances are, in this roulette of things, I shall
still be here, keying myself into daily enthusiasm
for the odds and ends of news in this harbor.
Beyond doubt I am lost, though at times I would
swear I am saved. These times are when I look
out over the water and see Chris Loch standing
to the oars in his tar-covered rowboat. He seems
to hold the solution to so much. The disease of
ambition has passed him by.

Why cannot I have the attitude of Chris
Loch? For certainly the country now has need
for no more celebrities. It should be everybody's
patriotic duty for awhile to remain humble.
Why must I, too, crave to be publicized, so publicized that the hotel clerks of each town will
know me when I register, so publicized that I
safely can say I do not care for publicity, and say
it without the risk of having the reporters (I'm
one) take me at my word. Time after time I
hold such debates with myself as I look out at
Chris Loch, and see him in the sunlight working
away immune from our opinions about him, and

see him thrilled at being his own captain, even if
of a rowboat.

His skin is of that Scandinavian lightness so
quick to tan, so quick to register the weather, so
sure of retaining red cheeks until right up to the
last day of old age.   But I do not think he is
Scandinavian.   I think he is Dutch.   And finally
I wrote the story on him.

I based the story on what type of articles he
most frequently dragged to the surface, and
where he sold them.   Old lines were what he
found mostly, old lines and hawsers lost overboard from tugs and freighters.   These he sold
to junk dealers and to mariners at so much a
pound, depending on the condition.   Sometimes
he hooked onto old anchors, once he found a
crate of bourbon. It had slipped overboard while
being transferred from a captured rum-runner
to a police truck.   And once he found a bicycle
which had fallen off the pier.   A messenger boy
had leaned the bicycle against a piling while he
boarded a Navy transport to deliver a telegram.
The bicycle whirled about of its own accord and
tumbled over the side. The old salvager dragged
for it and delivered it to the boy for the price of
a thank you.

Items such as these I put into my feature
story, and to make the paragraphs the more complete Chris happened to live in a diminutive

houseboat he had built from driftwood and from drift-logs. I put into the story—now that I think it over—not a tribute to him so much as a defense of myself. I belittled all my own secret desires to be something, somebody. I emphasized how he did not have to work except on those days when he desired to work, but if he did not work he could not eat so much. He was his own supply and demand, he personified the great equation between industry and needs. Personal publicity did not mean a thing to him, he did not know its meaning.

But, curious to see the effect his name in print would have for him, I took a copy of the paper to him. I did so rather guiltily, rather mindful of showing a happy animal its face in a mirror. He was aboard his houseboat at the time. He was seated on a rebuilt chair on what was equivalent to a veranda. But it was large enough only for a flower box and a chair. He was smoking. His day's work was ended, and he was looking off upon the shore.

The sun was at that hesitant moment just before setting, that curious moment when some of these evenings it will change its mind about setting from sight and will bob back up again. But this was not the night. Chris watched me as I neared the gangplank. He seemed to know I was coming to see him. His chair was tipped

against the patched wall.   He could have been
God reconsidering, during a spell of rest, the
world he had just created.

"Hello, Chris."

"Come down, eh."

The gangway was of one plank.   The tide was
out, so the gangway was steep.   For footing it
had crosspieces nailed unevenly.   No two pieces
were alike.

I carried the paper concealed in a roll beneath
my coat.   I would keep it in reserve for a minute
or two.   I would surprise him.   We would talk
first, then I would show him the story, I would
show him for the first time how his name looked
in print.

"Nice write-up, my fellow," he said.

"What, you've seen it!"   With difficulty I retained my balance on the sharp plank.   "You
mean you buy the paper?"

"Always when there is a write-up about me,
I buy it—always.   Yours already is in my scrapbook.   Ever seen my scrapbook?"

Where, then, on this waterfront is left an example of obscured and silent nobility upon which
I may lean?   Where?   Now that Chris has gone.
Now that he has deserted me.   Now that he, too,
is on the side of the enemy.

VII

I KNOW the skipper of the garbage boat pretty well. His boat is the *Abraham Lincoln,* and each morning he goes from destroyer to destroyer collecting the ships' garbage off the port aft deck.

The garbage is all piled up there waiting for him. There are crates, cartons, orange peelings, grapefruit peelings, all things like that.

The deck hands help push the stuff over the side into the little craft. The aft is rigged out with high side boards, and the stuff is shot down inside through a chute of canvas.

The skipper is Gus Valentino. He signs a contract with the Navy to do this sort of thing. The contract is obtained by bidding, and he is always the lowest bidder, for the *Abraham Lincoln* is not elaborate. No money is ever wasted on paint, and the motor long ago abandoned any notion about speed.

Once the load is aboard, the craft has till daybreak next morning to return. Nobody in port cares once the load is aboard and safely out of the harbor.

The sea gulls on each trip are so thick around

him that they blind the rickety craft in a pageant of white feathers. There are, in fact, times when the *Abraham Lincoln* is a cloud of sea gulls. They could be attached there by wires, he could be the invisible driver of a float in the Mardi Gras. He makes no attempt to frighten them away. He calls them hens, his hens. He knows, I guess, that he could not frighten them away if he did try. Experience would have taught them by now that he was only bluffing them. All of them try to ride, but there are too many. The majority have to fly, and as they fly they squawk. They have transformed this daily garbage-collecting from a job into a celebration.

Nobody need feel sorry for Valentino, either. At his home in the local community we call Lisbon he has nine children, and children can eat spaghetti which is cheap when made in a huge bowl. Nobody need feel sorry for Valentino anyway.

The other morning, for instance, he and his sea gulls were parading down the bay just as the flagship *Texas* entered port with the Commander-in-Chief aboard. The rails were manned by sailors at attention all along the line, and at the salute of the guns the garbage collector said: "This is another great day for the *Abraham Lincoln*. Another great day for the hens, and another great day for Valentino. For Valentino, you see, doesn't have to salute back."

VIII

MORE invigorating than any outside meetings we cover for the paper are the paper's own meetings for the staff. These meetings begin at four-thirty the Thursdays of each week unless postponed at four-thirty-five because the editors had forgotten the day was the day.

If the editors forget about the meeting, it goes off rather smoothly. We reporters, who have seen enough of the office anyway for that day, hang around somebody's typewriter until five telling each other how sore we are and how we are not going to show up at all for the meeting next Thursday if this sort of thing keeps up.

But when the editors do not forget about the meeting we carry our chairs into the chief's room. We sit against the wall, each of us quietly wondering why we are not syndicate writers for the chain, for their stuff is frightful lately, always has been frightful, and they can get by with more generalities in their copy than we can get by in our copy locally, and our New York columnist who is repeating himself really should get to work for a change and cover a beat.

He is getting by with murder and were it not for a pair of scissors he could not possibly catch the mails with his stuff. The heads must be blind to let his copy ride, and how in hell does a fellow become a syndicate writer anyway. By having an aunt who knows the chairman, that's how. And by having a chairman who doesn't read his own papers, and by having a power of speech to offset the lack of power of writing, and what in God's name was scheduled for the meeting today. To be sure, one of the copy readers is to talk on leads.

"Short, snappy leads, that's what we want—"

He is beginning, the copy reader is beginning with his talk, and it will not be long now before he tells us that the greatest story which ever broke, the one about the world, was told in seven "takes," and why doesn't that woman in the hotel over there take her exercises in front of the window any more. She used to be good about it, but the gang in the sports' department ruined her. That's what happened. They made too much noise watching. That new fellow did, anyway, and yet she has a right to bend in privacy if she wants to. Just like anybody else, maybe. Oh, yes, the copy reader is now telling about one of the greatest leads ever written, the one for the death of Theodore Roosevelt.

"It was one of the New York papers. I forget

which one, but its lead hit you smack in the face. 'Theodore Roosevelt is dead.' Just that. Nothing more on the first line. There's a sample of brevity that can't be beat, and I'd like to see more of you fellows around here try it—"

Try what? Oh, yes, try a story on Roosevelt dying. It's too bad we don't pay to attend these meetings. We really should pay something for all the advice we get here. It's a shame we get all this inspiration for nothing. We really should chip in each Thursday and make a pot. We wouldn't have to give much, but just a little to ease our conscience. But why doesn't somebody hurry and tell us again about the greatest editorial ever written on Christmas. It's not right to have us wait so long to have that editorial read to us again. Yes, Isabella Gladys Mary Johnson, there is a Santa Claus. You cannot see him or you cannot hear him, but he is with us all the time. Oh, why doesn't somebody hurry and read that editorial to us again. Christmas is too long to wait, and what is being passed around to us now?

To be sure, samples of news writing during the past month. Glorious. It looked for awhile as if somebody for once might have forgotten to pass around these samples, and that would have been too much to bear after a hard day like today. But what if, after all, he has forgotten the human-interest story about the dog awakening the family. Surely he will not forget that one, especially with so many fires of our own around here lately. And what if he has forgotten the one about the actress going on the stage despite her appendicitis.

"You will notice that in each of these clippings the reporter was not content with mere surface facts. He dug deeper. What normally would have passed as routine news of a paragraph he turned into little masterpieces that made the front page second section, and that's what we want to see more of. Don't be lazy, don't leave a stone unturned, don't just write what you know and leave it go at that. But see what this reporter's done. He used his imagination, that's what he did, and see how much brighter it is. He wasn't just content with the facts, but he wanted more. Now, that's what I want to see more of in you men, that's what'll make our paper stand out above the opposition—"

Why doesn't he hurry and tell us about keeping our desks cleaner? To be sure, it's ten minutes too early for that part. The keep-your-desks-cleaner doesn't come till after the don't-phone-long-distance-without-telling-the-phone-girl, and that doesn't come till after the altogether-too-much-running-in-and-out-of-the-office-between-editions, and that doesn't come till after the you'll-have-to-cut-it-out-spitting-in-the - wastebaskets - so - much - for - the - janitor - collects - those - old - papers.

And if this meeting isn't over with pretty soon, nobody will be left alive to put out tomorrow's sheet. We'll all have died from finding no place to throw our cigarette butts. In New York do they hold meetings, too? No, in New York the fellows all have separate offices with telephones, and in summer they go to France as correspondents, and when they want to go to a show they don't have to ask the managing editor for a Comp. No, they just phone up Belasco or Carroll— Hello, here comes the next speaker. Good, now we'll hear about the advantages of the women's page. Cheers for the women's page and all like it—

IX

TODAY I had to deliver a message to a young sailor aboard a destroyer anchored in the harbor. I had to inform him of what perhaps is the deepest news to a man, and I was conscious the while of a primitive curiosity of how he would weather the information.

Our office had received a wire story from Portland that the man's wife had attempted to kill herself and had succeeded in chloroforming to death her two children.

This, I knew, was the acme of all bad news. In my time I have delivered many verbal messages of death to wives and to husbands. But now I positively had the very worst, and I still wonder why I was not more ashamed of my own personal curiosity.

In sending me out to the vessel, the office, of course, was not being philanthropic. The wire service out of Portland wanted an interview with the sailor, wanted a story on him, wanted to know if he could explain any motive for the double crime. My own paper wanted the story, too. Being the waterfront reporter, I merely was the agent. For I did not know the man.

My shoreboat let me off at the gangway, and I asked the officer of the deck if I could see the sailor.

"A hell of a thing's happened to his family," I said. "And I have to tell him."

"Sure, if it's real important."

"It is."

The officer of the deck summoned an orderly, and the orderly went in search of the sailor, and in time the sailor arrived from below, smiling. From the helm and chevrons on his sleeve I could tell he was a quartermaster first-class, and I felt like God standing there with the power to crunch him. I was a giant with a fly-swatter. For all of his smile he could not get away from me. He was cornered.

The grief on my face was not all natural. Some of it was placed there professionally for the sake of the interview I should obtain from him without his really knowing. And from that moment on I was aware of having been in newspaper work a day too long. I, too, was gone the same as the desk men were gone, the desk men who had sent me out here.

"Does your family live in Portland?" I asked, to make sure.

"Yes."

"And have you two children?" I gave their names.

"Yes."

"Then come over here." I guided the way to the ship's railing. There we could lean and look down into the water. The bay would be our only audience. And all the time I was acting. I was breaking the news after the formula of the stage. I did not comprehend how I could be so indifferent, or how I could be thinking of my story as much as of him. I was preparing my interview ahead of time, and my face by now must be the face of a hard man. It must be hard, for I am hard. The test came and found me hard.

"Your wife attempted suicide."

He glanced quickly towards me, as if to catch me delivering a practical joke, almost as if to see if I would break into a laugh. But the reportorial actor in me continued to register sorrow. Convincing sorrow, too, perhaps. For immediately he depended on me for more information, and feeling this dependence I permitted my information to linger awhile. He would have demanded more outright, but I beat him to the words!

"But she's all right now. She didn't get by with it. But before trying to kill herself, she did—"

Now for the fly-swatter. Now for the execution. Was my prisoner ready? Was he in the proper suspense. Yes, he was ready. He was waiting. Very well, then let him have it. And watch his expression too. And catch each little word he may say. You'll need it, waterfront reporter. You'll need it to write for the desk men. And they'll need it for Portland. You're on a job, don't forget. The shoreboat to send you out here cost money, good money. Let him have it. Let the young man have it now.

"But before trying to kill herself, she did—" And I came down with the swatter. And back in the office my story made the front page, my story carried a head reserved for human-interest stories, and the managing editor said the story "showed the good old stuff." I know, because he commented on the story in staff meeting. He said the story got down under the surface and had "all the good old sympathy guts to it that I want to see more of around here."

X

FOR washing the city off one's skin at the end of a day's work, nothing around here of course quite equals a fast dive into the surf when few people are present on the beach. Many are present at noon, but not at the end of the day, for the summer visitors usually prefer their dips when the sun is at its highest pitch for tanning the Eastern shoulders.

My favorite cove, then, usually is rather deserted near supper-time, and I can dive for all I like without the danger of seeming to be showing off.

The rollers come in regularly, are hushed a bit by a reef, and can be timed to one's liking. Each seventh roller usually is the largest. It puffs out its blue chest in defiance to its enemy, the beach, which so soon will put an end to all such gallantry.

The roller comes on, begins to show a white curl along the top as though showing its teeth at the sand, and then is the time to strike, and to strike straight for the stomach of the brute.

By opening one's eyes, then, the under-water world is such a contrast to the upper world that

all of the day's ridiculous transactions are in-
stantly slashed off the register of one's brain.
A few rocks are down there, to be sure, but they
are more like under-water benches, and they are
upholstered with waving seagrass.   And from
under the legs of these benches the golden
Garibaldi perch poke their surprised heads out
to see what is happening, or has happened, and
so odd is all this new room to the world-house
that one for a time does not really miss the
inability to breathe.

But late in the afternoon recently my cove has
been having a group of visitors, the same visitors now for five successive evenings.   Two
women are in the group and two men.   And one
of the men, the one who appears about my own
age, has been doing his swimming almost constantly in the one clear spot for diving. He stays
there, swimming about on his back, sometimes
floating, sometimes paddling, but always in the
way.   He seldom leaves the shoreline more than
a few yards, and I have to wait for him.   He does
not dive under the water, nor does he seem much
interested in what is down there, the greens and
yellows, the abalone shells, and the few Garibaldi.

Frequently I have been tempted to dive in
close to him, or under him, just to teach him a
few manners.   And once when we were both out

there and I was trying to get by him for deeper water he swam right into me from a crazy angle.

"Pardon me," he said, and continued paddling on his back. But I was too annoyed at his awkwardness to answer civilly. I mumbled something and swam on.

Later, about twenty minutes later, when I returned to the sand to go home, the other people were getting ready to go home, too. And I watched them climb the trail leading up the cliff. They were guiding the young man along, the man who was about my own age. For, his eyes being open and as clear as my own, I had not known he was blind, completely blind. And when I open my eyes under water now, and see the room of retreat down there, I feel kind of funny. I feel kind of funny and shaky all over.

XI

ON that future winter night when my children's children gather on the floor around me and ask: "Please, dear Granddaddy, tell us of your most miserable assignment," I shall describe to them my sardine-fishing trip on the little sardine-boat *Mió Jesus*.

I asked the skipper of the boat if he would take me out with him sometime, and he said he would "sometime." I asked him if he would take me out that very same night and he answered, "No, not tonight." I asked him why, and he answered that he could not tell me why. And so that is how it came to pass that I went out with him. For at eight-thirty that evening I boarded his little vessel, and at nine he came aboard and found me there.

"How-do, Mr. Mederna."

He replied: "Huh. Hello." He continued on into the pilot house and left me alone on the aftdeck to entertain myself. This seemed odd of him, as we had known each other several years and he had always been wanting to repay me somehow for the time I ran his daughter's picture as queen of the Portuguese festival.

The sardines had not been running so well this season, all of which may have accounted in part for his low spirits. And I would have stepped ashore again except that his men right then cast off the lines and the little vessel started under way.

A high haze hid the stars as by a veil, and the crew seemed glad of this, as the blacker the night the better the sardine fishing. The men continued working with the nets until the *Mió Jesus* was well out of the channel, then the skipper motioned me to come into the pilot house.

"You might as well go below and sleep," he said. "When we spot a school I'll call you."

His voice was more of a command than an invitation, leaving nothing for me to do except to climb down into the forecastle and to crawl into the first bunk. The blankets smelled of fish, as these fishermen do not always remove their clothes before turning in for a sleep between watches, and I could imagine seeing fish scales glistening out at me through the darkness. My head became blurred with the odor and the pitch of the vessel. But I did not become sick, not then, although I did doze as though under the influence of a disagreeable and light dose of ether.

Later I was partly aroused by what sounded like the scraping of our starboard fenders against the hull of another vessel. The porthole in the forecastle was well forward of my bunk, and I was too uncomfortable in my stomach to dare get up to look out. Staying right where I was, I soon passed off into another siege of dizziness and remained that way for what may have been an hour or two hours or three hours.

The captain's voice awakened me. He was calling down into the forecastle: "Hi-ho, we're getting action."

I came out on deck, and far aft of us was a lantern rising and falling with the roll of the ocean. The lantern was our own and marked the end of the net the men were heaving overboard as fast as they could. Our little vessel began swinging to starboard and was completing a great circle back to the floating lamp. This was the way, then, the sardines were captured. They were corralled, and the observation pleased me as much as though the method were my own discovery.

The sardines school to our starboard was nothing more than a wide sheet of phosphorescence. A man on the bow was signalling with his arms to Mederna at the wheel. The two men had to work fast as the school was likely to dart in any direction which pleased its fancy.

We completed the circle back to the lantern, and the men began drawing the lampar-net into a pocket. One end of the net was being drawn aboard, and the captive sardines began kicking a fuss in earnest now. The darkness of the skies exaggerated the phosphorescent flames which shot from their tiny bodies.

When the net was drawn as tightly into a pocket as it could be drawn without squeezing the sardines to pieces, another net of fine mesh and shaped much like a huge bucket was lowered over the side by a hand-crane. This bailer was dipped down into the sardines, then hauled back aboard again. Sheafs of water poured from it, and the sardines were emptied on deck. The bailer dipped again into the sea and brought up another load, and another, and another. The sardines were raining upon us, and nowhere could we hide to get away from them.

"Here," the skipper said to me, "put on these hip boots. You'll need them." I needed them all right, for by now the sardines were up to my knees. The whole thing had turned into a sardine-blizzard. A man passed a line into my hand. On the end of the line was a stone. He told me to put the stone over into the net and to keep moving it up and down. The reason either was to frighten the sardines deeper into the net or to frighten them up from the bottom. The reason was explained to me but I have forgotten. All I know is that I had to work, and that the more I worked the more acute became my stomach-trouble. So many sardines all at once were beginning to influence me, and the crisis to my illness came when I had to bow my head over the side to work the stone.

The sardines were up to our hips now, and whenever we wanted to move we had to wade through them as through snow. Sardines dropped down into the opening of our boots and wiggled there, but we could not stoop to drag them out or another avalanche would be upon us. I said the hell with trying to be a feature writer of sardines. I said the hell with everything. I wanted to go home. I wanted no more sardines, but the captain did, and so we continued. And when the decks appeared to be unable to hold more, the captain ordered side boards placed upon the side boards already there, and the work went on.

When next I was able to raise my head through the snowbank of sardines, a peculiar change was coming over the world. The sky had turned from black to a dirty gray, and the phosphorescence had faded from the net. This, then, was the coming of that famous dawn we always read so much about. And with dawn came a call from our port. We turned and saw another vessel closing in on us. The vessel bore on its bow the numbers of a Coast Guard vessel.

I recognized the Coast Guard officer, a chief boatswain, and he recognized me despite my hip boots and despite my sudden change of stomachs. He should have recognized me all right, considering the many times I had interviewed him during past years. I called to him up on the bridge: "Mr. Lundstrom, you're going to have a passenger. I'm it."

"Why, hello there," he said right back. "I thought your place was ashore at a typewriter."

"It is and I want to get there as soon as I can." But before saying any more, I had to take time out over the side of the vessel to demonstrate my earnestness. This completed, I continued: "Come about two feet closer and I can jump it."

"I'll come closer, all right. In fact, I'll have to search the boat. Sorry."

I asked him what he meant and he explained that during the night some craft had made contact with the mother ship off the coast. He said he was searching everything that floated. I told him to spare the trouble here as I had been aboard all night.

"Jump across then, son, and we'll be on our way. I've plenty to do other places, God knows."

What more to say about the matter puzzles me, although I have thought about the whole thing a great deal since then. In the excitement of the sardines and in the excitement of my own misery, I sincerely had forgotten at the time about the odd hospitality of Mederna and about hearing our starboard fenders scrape in the middle of the night. But I do know for certain that I saved the *Mió Jesus* for Mederna and his crew. I know for certain because he thanked me three days later, and he gave me six bottles in a gunnysack.

"What can you do?" he asked. "What can you do when sardines are only bringing twenty dollars the ton?"

"You mean you only get twenty dollars a ton for all that?"

He said: "Yes. And that night you were with us was the first time all week we had caught any. The first time all week—friend."

XII

WHENEVER the Navy's submarine rescue vessel returns to port from practice outside, I make an effort to eat lunch aboard her. I do not eat there to obtain information about deep-sea diving (because I am weary of obtaining information about deep-sea diving), but I like to eat there because one of the divers is having trouble with a former wife. She comes aboard to collect what perhaps is alimony.

About four or five years ago the little vessel with all its divers and its diving suits was what might be called "interesting." When feature stories were scarce the vessel always could be depended on for copy of some sort with which to appease the masters. There was (and still is) her pipe organ on the bridge for supplying air to the divers. There were the divers themselves. There were the salvage pontoons with all their bulk, and all of which was exciting five years ago. But this attitude has all worn away now not to be revived until a new young man takes my place fifty years from today.

The vessel's decompression chamber was what fascinated me the most, and in my enthusiasm of old I even sat inside of it to be decompressed after having made a dive of my own. In my dive no encounters were made with octopi or sharks or pirates' chests. Nothing occurred to make the dive worth talking about. All I did was to be lowered on the diving-stage and to hang around the bottom for awhile. The demonstration more than anything was simply another proof that the world does not need me, and that I may as well be down on the bottom as any other place. Nobody objected to the length of my stay.

On being hoisted to the surface on the diving-stage, assistants known as "bears" seized the equipment off me and rushed me into the decompression chamber. All the divers are handled this way after going down forty feet or more. Sometimes they have to stay in the chamber only an hour and sometimes four or five hours, depending on how long they have been working on the bottom.

The chamber itself does not provide much in the way of entertainment. It is nothing more than a large air-proof tank lying on its side in the starboard of the vessel. The chamber is too small to stand in, so the diver sits on a stool or on the floor, or sometimes he has a cot moved in and sleeps there. Food, water and medical supplies can be passed in through a series of trap-doors while the pressure is still on, but the divers become pretty sick of the place after the first two or three years.

The high pressure of the chamber also makes the men a bit drunk, especially the new divers. Their sight becomes a bit cockeyed, their sense of distances is bad, and they frequently get to giggling over nothing at all. They can be watched from the outside through a thick plate glass the size of a porthole, but they usually prefer being left alone until their time is up. Their diving suits have been left outside to be patched and dried, and the men sit inside in their heavy diving underwear.

The diver having trouble with his former wife has been diving for sixteen years. He has worked on the East coast, the West coast and in the Asiatics. He knows all the tricks. Once he found a diamond ring which had been lost off a pier by a woman. She had lost the ring while waving her hand to some marines leaving on a transport. She remembered exactly where she was standing at the time, and the diver said he would go down and try to find the stone.

Although a ladder reached down the side of the pier he would not go down the ladder. He chose to go out in one of the Navy's small diving-boats and to walk back towards the pier against the current. In this way the mud stirred by his heavy shoes would flow away from the ring instead of over it. He found the ring almost immediately, but he stayed down there thirty or forty minutes longer pretending he still was searching. He did not want the job to appear too easy.

When finally he signalled to be brought up she was as grateful as could be over the ring's recovery. She invited him and his two helpers to her apartment for dinner, and later they went to a picture show as her guests. After awhile he began visiting her without the company of the helpers.

The Navy discourages most enlisted men from becoming married because their wages are too small, but chiefs are all right. He was a chief torpedo-man, the Navy having no diver ratings, and he and she were married until about two years ago. She obtained a divorce then and an agreement concerning finances. They have no children, but her lawyer obtained a monthly settlement of fifty-two dollars from him.

She likes him to be regular with his payments and is still threatening to take him to court. He is three months behind now, and so when the vessel returns to the harbor she comes aboard to visit him. The crew treats her politely, for when she becomes annoyed she has access to words which the men themselves are sensitive about utilizing for fear of court-martial. But her

interviews with her former husband have till
now been rather unsuccessful.   On being informed by the sailor on watch that "She's
coming out the pier," the diver runs into the
decompression chamber and bolts the door behind him.

While inside there he shifts his regular clothes
for his heavy diving underwear, and by all ap-
pearances he is very tired from a long siege on
the bottom. She does not know about the speaking tube or she could talk with him. But the
men have not told her of the tube, and the best
she can do is stand outside the thick plate glass
and denounce him with gestures.

The men have been nice in explaining to her
the workmanship of the chamber, and how if he
were to be taken out ahead of time he would receive an attack of the bends and might die. This
reference to bends is true, of course, and she
could not help but know of the danger of the
disease. For it is frightful, being air bubbles
which enter a diver's veins if he has been hoisted
to the surface without decompression. She
understands this, but she cannot understand why
he should always be inside the chamber when she
comes aboard.

"Because, ma'am," the men repeat to her, "because, ma'am, he is our best diver and so always
goes down deeper than the rest of us."

"Deeper? But how can he go deeper if you're all diving at the same place? Don't the rest of you all go to the bottom, too?"

"No—yes, ma'am. But you see we go out to a deeper place just for him. The Navy wants to keep him in special practice."

"It's a lie."

"As you like, ma'am. But you can write the Navy Department."

This suggestion she apparently has not taken. But she has demanded an answer to how long he must stay in there, and this answer always comes back in technical phraseology. He must stay in there according to the decompression tables which roughly amount to twice or thrice the time he has been on the bottom, all depending on whether he was desaturated any on his way to the surface. This explanation is confusing to her, although the men are always careful not to leave out any mathematical details. She wants to know how long he will be in there this time, and for the men to come to the point, to come to the point. This is her favorite phrase, this phrase of come to the point.

The men endeavor to come to the point, their estimates varying from four more hours to maybe a week, ma'am, and would she care to wait. She has cared to wait, any number of times she has cared to wait. But the diver can as easily wait too. For food is passed in to him through the trapdoors, nor is he under any pressure whatever. No pressure has been turned into the chamber, and the air is the same as in any other part of the vessel.

If ever she should learn this fact, a possible climax to the affair might come if she should snoop around until she found the valves controlling the chamber's pressure. She could turn on this pressure full force, and her former husband would be in a devil of a fix then. But so far this has not happened and, like so many incompleted stories down here on the waterfront, perhaps never will. I may as well stop visiting the vessel, I guess.

XIII

Hello, you old sub-chaser," I whisper each time I see her. For she is my war vessel. We have a secret.

She operates out of port here with the Coast Guard fleet, but once she was in the regular Navy, and usually when I see her she is fast to the embarcadero taking on water and stores.

To be sure, there is not much of her to see. She is of wood, and the only apparent change from war days is that her galley has been moved amidships from aft.

The grandest holiday I ever had was during the war. I was aboard this vessel.

I turned eighteen just in time to enlist. All talk, of course, was of U-boats. And being from inland Montana I naturally chose the Navy.

At our training camp in Bremerton, a call came one day for forty volunteers to man a fleet of sub-chasers. Presuming that they would take us immediately to the North Sea, I stepped from the squads so fast that I guess I was the first person out there. The results were lesson enough for me not to volunteer again for anything, but simply to let matters take their course.

A person always gets there just as soon. Even sooner, for every fellow in that training camp eventually reached European waters except the forty who volunteered.

The sub-chasers were months and months being launched, and more months and months being fitted. We had to stand guard around them, and as we stood guard we could see our former companions in the training camp march past the board walk to join battleships, transports and destroyers.

The war was being fought, yet there we stayed, doing guard duty around our sub-chasers which never would be ready. And whenever there was a Liberty Bond drive we were marched out to parade for it, and always we had persons ask us which ship we were from. Every last man of us, I do believe, was close to suicidal. We even held secret arguments about what would happen to us if we deserted to join the Army under fictitious names.

The delay was intolerable, then suddenly one morning we sailed.

As often happens after an intolerable wait, the actual sailing orders caught us off guard. Our vessels were not fully equipped, and our officers were fresh from school. We had not seen them before they came aboard, and they had not seen us. They were as inexperienced as we were, and they frankly admitted it. At least our skipper admitted it. He was an ensign, barely in his twenties, and as agreeable as could be. He had joined the officers' class directly from university, and on that chilly morning when we first struck the sea out of Puget Sound he was the first to get seasick. But we liked him. He was so frank about how little he knew, and theoretically he did know enough about navigation to keep us away from shore. Also he was curious about visiting new ports as we were. He stopped at as many as he dared. The need for fresh water and vegetables always served as the excuse. For our refrigerator was no more than an ice box, and as for fresh water, it was a problem.

Along the Mexican coast we visited San José del Cabo and Acapulca. The sea here was luke-warm for swimming, and bumboats came out to the sub-chaser with bananas to sell. The whole thing was glorious, the whole thing was new. We played as hard as we could, reminding ourselves that we would pay for it all when we reached the frigid North Sea. We put into Corinto and we put into Balboa. The fools among us were left there in the Navy hospital, in the isolated ward. The survivors sailed on. From Colon we crossed the Caribbean to Guantanamo. We went from Havana to Key West, and there left more of our men in the hospital, again in the isolated ward, the young ensign with them. He had survived the Central American ports but Havana had caught him.

A new commander came aboard. He was more experienced with sea and with ports, and he took us to Newport. From there we would cross to Europe. The orders were written and ready, but something held us up. It was the war, it was ending—and it ended. It ended right while we were standing-by to go.

As a result I know nothing of war's grimness, and though I spent two years in the Navy I dare not call myself a war veteran. The cruise was the happiest experience I ever had, and I am ashamed that in some way I cannot repay the Government for the trip. The best I can do is to keep silent now when I look at my old vessel in port here.

Yes, it returned to the West coast, and was one of the few sub-chasers not sold to fishermen or millionaires. I wish I were not so ashamed to look at it—my war. I wish it would go somewhere else to spend its last days. For I did have such a good time aboard her, the little war-ghost. I wish it would clear out and give my conscience a rest.

"Hello, you little sub-chaser," I whisper. "Do, for God's sake, get out." But it doesn't. It simply pretends not to hear.

XIV

ONE morning the bow of a freighter up from the Canal Zone plowed into the side of our new pier. The bow tore out two pilings and cracked the cement.

The damage would cost plenty, and this was the second pier the captain had rammed already that year. Both times the tide had caught him wrong, and the stern lines had snapped the second he needed them most.

I found him aboard in his cabin. He was sitting there waiting while the harbor master made an estimate of the damage. The harbor master had gone back to his office, and the captain was alone when I found him.

I started to tell him how sorry I was, but he interrupted me: "Say, a little thing like that doesn't disturb me, boy. Life's too brief to be disturbed about anything. No, don't let anything ever disturb you. Take it from a man who knows. Take it from me."

"All right, all right," I promised him. But he was not through advising me.

"No," he continued, "there's no use letting anything get you down. What happens is just too bad. But forget about it. Things will average up in time. After all, there's no sense in letting anything get you down. Hell, no. Life's too brief to let a little mishap get you down. By the next day, now, you'll have forgotten all about it. Sure, by the next day you'll have forgotten all about it, boy. Isn't that right?"

He waited for an answer, so I nodded that it was right.

"Sure it's right," he continued. "Anybody but a fool would know it was right. Nothing's worth worrying about. You remember my words, boy."

In time I left him, still talking, and I hurried back to the paper to turn in my copy for the noon edition. While I was pushing the typewriter the police reporter telephoned in to the desk that the police ambulance had just returned from a rush job to the waterfront. The captain of the freighter was in a bad way. He had shot at his heart, missing it by a fraction.

He had been talking to himself, then, instead of to me.

XV

TODAY I helped Eddie Tarantino be midwife to a woman tourist from Wyoming, and tonight my emotions continue to bubble over like Seltzer water.

"Pooh," I try to calm myself, "what's one more baby more or less?" Yet my emotions continue to bubble over anyhow.

All premature babies, I had presumed, were born on farms usually in February. The farmer would harness his horses and go galloping through snowdrifts in search of the town doctor who would not be home.

But this birth of Eddie's and mine occurred under a warm sun and aboard the shoreboat which runs between the pier and the fishing barge outside. The run requires about an hour each way, depending on the tides and on the pitch of the sea beyond the channel.

The first fishing party usually leaves town at eight each morning. Eddie makes his first run then, another at noon, and another at sunset. The passengers are mostly strangers from inland anxious to catch a deep-sea fish before returning to their distant homes. Bamboo poles and meals

are furnished them on the barge, also live-bait
sardines. The passengers need to bring only
themselves and possibly their cameras. As a
result the shoreboat usually is filled with every
type of person, men, women and children.

Eddie has learned to answer their many questions automatically while standing at the wheel.
He does not turn around to talk with the passengers, and he does not like to be bothered
taking the tickets. He is always asking some
friend to come along and do this for him, the
payment being the ride. How many times I have
put to sea at his request I do not know, but this
morning was one too much, and never again do
I want to look at his shoreboat or at the fishing
barge either, having reached the conclusion tonight that I have seen enough of both.

Neither of us paid any more attention to the
woman when she came aboard than we would
pay to any other stout woman. She was wearing a coat, and she was one of sixteen other
passengers who boarded the shoreboat at the
pier.

The first attention we paid to her she attracted
to herself by not leaving the shoreboat when we
reached the fishing barge. The other passengers
climbed immediately aboard the barge, each
passenger anxious to seize a pole and make a
catch before the others made one. But this
woman would not budge from her seat.

"Aren't you going to fish, ma'am?" Eddie asked, waiting for her to rise.

She shook her head: "I ain't feeling none too well."

We noticed her condition then for the first time, and presumed that the waves were what had aggravated her. Eddie swung the boat around and started back to port, still having no idea she was as far along as she was, although he has seven youngsters of his own in Little Italy. We tried not to pay attention to her, fearing she would be embarrassed. I stood with Eddie at the wheel giving her full freedom of the aft-deck.

The shoreboat pitched, to be sure, yet everything would calm down as soon as we crossed the channel bar. But this apparently was not soon enough.

"Boys, don't go so rough," she said. "I'm expecting."

"Yes, ma'am," Eddie answered. "We'll be careful. We'll be past the worst in a minute."

He did not know, of course, that she was expecting so soon, nor did she or she would not have taken the ride. This seemed reasonable, and we tried to forget about her by not looking at her even when she talked.

After awhile she called again, and this time her voice had such desperation in it that Eddie left the wheel to me. He hurried back to her and tried to make her comfortable on the bench along the gunwale. But this was not large enough to do. He hurried forward down into the locker room and brought up all the clothes and things he could find. By clearing away the passenger seats he prepared a bed for her down on the deck.

"Open the engine for all it's got," he called to me. "To hell with the waves." He stayed back there with her talking for all he was worth. She tried to talk, too, and together they made as much noise as the motor. I was afraid to turn around, and started looking for help. The nearest vessel was a tuna-clipper chugging back into port behind us with a load aboard and not going half as fast as our own shoreboat. The clipper would be no help. But we did reach the protection of the channel. The seas died down, and I felt sure that everything would be all right now. But, to the contrary, everything reached a climax just inside the bar. There was no talking behind me now, but only moans and a lot of hard breathing, Eddie breathing as hard as she.

Once he came forward, grabbed the wire-clippers from the toolbox, and without a word to me he hurried back aft again. The shoreboat was travelling so fast through the calmness of the channel that I dare not take my eyes off the course, and this perhaps was a mighty saving factor for me. As soon as we reached the bay proper, the pier like a gentleman started coming out halfway to meet us. The spray from our bow was flying against our windows, and I did hope I would know how to dock the boat properly after such speed.

From the way our boat was cutting the water the helpers on the tugboat pier must have suspected something was wrong, for two of the men remained standing there staring.

Eddie called orders to me: "Don't bother making the boat fast. Let them do it. You go call the ambulance."

His voice was so authoritative that my first impulse was to answer: "Yes, sir." But instead I answered: "Righto," which perhaps is not the proper expression to use when a baby has just been born. Yet in either event life now holds no more surprises. I have helped in childbirth, I am he who held the wheel.

XVI

TWENTY-EIGHT comes quickly, all right. Thirty-eight will probably come quickly too. Yet I wonder if in between somewhere I shall become married. Probably, for all newspapermen eventually do become married, even waterfront reporters.

Marriage opens entirely new worlds for us, we are told by unmarried women who should know better than to become engaged to us either officially or unofficially. Marriage broadens our outlook and may be just the thing we need for humanizing our lives into lives of understanding instead of cynicism.

We should have children to greet us after our work in the office. Through watching them we may acquire that great sympathy of mankind so essential if ever we are to write our way out of newspaper bondage. We should become married, grow flowers, mow our lawns and love our neighbors. That, we are told by unmarried women, is the gateway to escape.

But by now I too might be married except for an early tragedy in my newspaper life, and a tragedy which still continues despite all my mental efforts to overcome it. And my tragedy also is a woman. She is married, and to another reporter in the office. He is older than I by about ten years, and his children total four, William, Elizabeth, Stephen and James.

I have watched them grow. In fact the whole office has watched them grow. We watched them grow several months before each was born, and they constantly have been before us ever since. We see them on the Saturday of each week, Saturday being our pay day, and the mother brings them to us then.

She seats them on the chairs outside the railing, two children to a seat, and the third chair next to the door is her own. There they remain quietly and uncomplainingly from ten-thirty until eleven when the girl from the business office brings the pay envelopes upstairs. The wife then arises and carefully blocks the passage until the girl finds the envelope destined for the man. The wife takes the envelope, turns and departs downstairs again, her fleet of four trailing after her.

No objection can be made to these Saturday visits because the wife does not literally interfere with the office's efficiency. She is careful to stay outside the railing and she is careful not to make a noise, and at home in the mornings she undoubtedly frightens the children to behave as they should by threatening not to take them with her for Papa's envelope.

The act has been going on now over so long a period, on so many pay days, on the same stage setting, before the same audience, that secretly I have constructed a drama around it merely to add variety. Yet because this family scene should be an inspiration to those of us in the office still unmarried, the drama I have created may seem on face value a little cruel. But cruelty is not the object of the drama. Rather the object, as stated before, is merely to add variety.

The scene opens with the wife arriving at her usual time of ten-thirty. Her larvæ arrive with her and are duly seated for the half-hour wait. The husband at his typewriter continues slaving at his routine copy. Not a sound or gesture of recognition passes between him and his family. All is as it has been during these many many other Saturdays.

Exactly at eleven the girl arrives upstairs from the business office with her box of envelopes. The wife arises and blocks the way as usual. The girl searches for this envelope first and hands it to the woman. But the only change between this day and the other days is that just as the wife is reaching for the envelope the husband quietly takes a revolver from the upper drawer of his desk and shoots the woman between the eyes.

She falls backward straight as a plank, her arm continuing to reach rigidly outward and upward as she falls.   And in falling straight backward she knocks over her four duplicates behind her as a row of cards.   They too fall over backwards respectively according to sizes, and there they lie, the five of them, while the husband returns the revolver to his drawer and resumes his typewriting.

This drama has been visualized for so long in my mind that on each Saturday I cannot understand why the scene does not take place. Vision and reality have become so confused that I cannot comprehend why the reporter continues his typewriting while she accepts the envelope and departs.   The man is not performing at all according to the lines which I, the dramatist, have prepared for him.   But on the day he does perform according to the lines, on that day and no other shall I become married.   So speaks Mohammed the prophet.   So speaks Mohammed, the founder of Islam.

XVII

WHILE other men are writing of Tibet and of China and of Africa and of India and of Suva and of Tahiti and of Mongolia, here I am trying to write of the diminutive islands south of here, islands which are immaterial and which will cause nobody to exclaim: "What—you haven't been there! Not really."

But yes, I have been there—really. Nor did the assignment constitute my idea of being a travel writer. In my travels I wanted to wear a suit of duck whites, a tropical hat, and carry a cane of carved bamboo. Women passengers would elbow women passengers, whispering: "But he's written more than travel books too. He's a great novelist."

"Not him."

"Yes, him."

But the space on these tuna-clippers is occupied, not by nudging women, but by chipped ice and by tanks of live-bait sardines. I could have worn a white suit. There is no law against it, but I would have had to scrub the suit myself each night. These Portuguese fishermen are dear fellows, all of them, yet they do not understand my love of white suits. And as for their own washing they prefer to wait until returning to port weeks later and there have their women do it.

As for the travel-copy, my favorite island remains Guadalupe with its elephant seals and with its thousands of goats gone wild. The complete story about these goats cannot be written for the paper because of the Christians on the subscription list. For these goats are being utilized for purposes not strictly moral. A small herd was first brought to the island a hundred years ago for a mission colony. The colony disappeared but the goats thrived among the rocky hillsides. The animals became wild and they increased and their number now is beyond count.

Two men live on the island the year around now. I know them from previous trips. We know each other so well that they confided exactly what they are doing. Each day they corral thirty goats by a spring on the side of a canyon. They kill only the billy goats, skinning them and curing them right there. The jerked meat they sell to the Mexican Army, the hides are sold to a concern in the United States, and those parts of the goats which the Mexican Army does not want the men grind into fine powder and sell to China. The Chinese feel they need this powder for reasons aphrodisiac and will pay any price for it.

But the service of the goats is not limited to China. Each year the yacht of a wealthy old man comes to anchor at Guadalupe. He has built a cabin high in the hills where the goats are the thickest. He says that the odorament of the goats makes him young again and that as far as he is concerned they do not have to be sacrificed. They are service enough just the way they are, alive, and can keep their glands. He brings his wife with him from Philadelphia. She is young and each year she wears a different face.

The man is too old and too rich to lug his own supplies from the yacht up the cliff to the concealed cabin. His crew does this for him and sometimes the two men on the island help. The old man pays them for it and also pays them to keep secret the name of the yacht. This secrecy, of course, has remained unbroken to this very day. For the only people who know of him are the two men who live on the island and the crews and skippers of the tuna fleet and their families and friends. Yet not for worlds would I have mentioned the subject either, except that the information should be passed on somehow to all other old men, and not be retained exclusively by the Chinese, and by this man from Philadelphia.

XVIII

THE harbor was discovered in 1542 by Cabrillo. The harbor was discovered in 1542 by Cabrillo. The harbor was discovered in 1542 by Cabrillo—

This phrase has come to be as much a part of me as, Now is the time for all good men to come to the aid of their party. The phrase about Cabrillo must be used twice a year and turned into a feature story, once for the winter annual and once for the summer annual.

By closing my eyes and using the touch system exclusively I can write the rest of the harbor's history too, from the time of Cabrillo "to the present thriving beehive of shipping industry." Some day while preparing this semi-annual story for the paper I shall become wise. I shall prepare a hundred carbon copies and file them away for the subsequent fifty years, two each year.

More copies may be needed. Yet this is doubtful. For waterfront reporters as a rule do not live to be more than eighty-five, and around there sometime is when I shall be presented with my cigarette-lighter for being the oldest living employee.

The reason these carbon copies were not prepared before is because I did not expect to be still here for the next annual. I always depended on Kismet (the word we poets use for Fate) to step in somehow and finish a book for me, after which I would be invited to New York as a columnist. Not an ordinary columnist, but a columnist who can write with dots, long rows of dots between words. I am good at dots. I have practiced dots a good many years now, although they do not blend so well when writing about mackerel and barracuda, and they usually have to be cut out before turning in my copy. The copy-desk is discouraging about dots. The desk prefers verbs and nouns and things like that.

Cabrillo discovered the harbor in 1542 while searching for gold. He sailed into the harbor and came ashore. He claimed all the land for Spain. And because all Spanish explorers must kneel on one knee and kiss the earth if ever they expect to have their pictures copied in textbooks while discovering, I always make a pretty description of this in my annual stories. In fact I am at my best in this special paragraph about Cabrillo.

I have the sun forming a resemblance of a halo over the locks of his hair, and the Pulitzer news-story prize committee should in time start noticing this paragraph. I cannot keep underlining it each time I mail the story East. Somebody on the committee should see it soon, for my modesty rebels against the thought of having to go there in person and read my story aloud to the members. They might become catty about my gestures, and might object in terms that the Cabrillo discovery, although important, no longer is exactly spot news, having reached the Spanish press first. This constant cry for speed, speed, speed, speed is what drives us newspapermen crazy, and which is the reason I always say to young men who ask my advice about entering journalism: "Stay out of it . . . stay out of it. . . . My God. . . ." And please just notice those dots.

XIX

HE used to live on the waterfront all the time, but not now. He left us a year ago in the spring to take a whale around the country in a box car.

The box car was specially made, being long and with lettering on the side: CAPTIVE WHALE. This lettering, of course, was an exaggeration which the man himself realized and which he was asked about in each city. Patrons who had paid their twenty-five cents frequently would demand an explanation why the whale, if it was a captive whale, also was not a live whale.

"My land, Mister," the man would answer, "you don't expect us to carry around a live whale in a train, do you?" The man was so practiced in his speech that he made his persecutors feel silly. He told us all about his speech when he returned.

He obtained his whale from the Scandinavian whaling fleet outside. One of the killer-ships brought the whale into port forty-eight hours dead, and the man helped the embalmers do the work.

103

They cut their way through to the whale's heart and they cut the heart out, the heart weighing twelve hundred pounds. They drained the two-inch arteries of their thousand gallons of blood and they soaked the whale with ten thousand gallons of embalming fluid. The figures are all familiar to me as I had to write them in a feature story.

In doing the feature story for the man not only was I made to feel a part of the whale-conspiracy but also he invited me to look at the whale any time I wished for nothing, "and to bring your lady friend along too if you got one."

The whale on its private train stood up well as far as Texas, then began to shrink. The man told us he was desperate for awhile but finally decided on what he calls "face-lifting." He inoculated the whale all over with hot paraffin. He shot the stuff down under the surface at each yard or so. The skin swelled back to its natural size and assumed the luster needed for his successful season in Cleveland, Atlantic City, Chicago, St. Paul, Baltimore, Buffalo and Detroit.

To us who have remained back here on the waterfront he can recite the cities quite rapidly, putting all the names in one. Before going with the whale he used to live in the abandoned watchman's hut by the tuna-cannery, but now he lives in an apartment uptown.

His picture sitting in the mouth of the whale has appeared in so many Eastern papers that he no longer seems one of us. He occasionally comes down to the waterfront to show us his scrapbook, then he goes back uptown again.

XX

EACH year a drive is held for funds to support the four-masted windjammer here in port, and in speaking of the windjammer I almost automatically preceded the word with the adjective old, being so accustomed to doing so in my newspaper copy about the vessel. The two words apparently always must go together, even though this vessel was built comparatively recently, and many of today's fanciest liners were built soon after.

But my paper, of course, takes part in the community drive. And, being the waterfront reporter, my assignment is to tell of the vessel's history. I must work myself up into a lather of sentimentality over sailing ships in general and this one in particular, and no circus press agent ever felt a greater damning of the soul.

This windjammer, to be sure, has all the markings of antiquity. Her paint is gone, her deck is bruised and her holds have the mustiness of a thousand years. But this is not because of wear and tear but because she has been standing around so much in port, moored to the same pier, never going anywhere. And if vessels, like men, could put on flesh by laziness this vessel would have been fat long before now and would have a double stomach and a double chin and would spend its days in a wicker chair garbling about the prowess of the years gone by.

True, the vessel took one cruise to Australia, but that was about all. The history of no sailing craft, though, can be written without giant storms, and the storms which this barkentine encountered on that trip to Australia grow larger and more numerous each year at fund-campaign time.

But I often have wondered why sailing vessels, like dogs, must never be under-sentimentalized. Should a reporter dare do this, the public for sure would write letters to the editor, and the reporter would be damned for having horns beneath his hat and hooves within his shoes. Nor during campaign time must we reporters hint that the construction of this windjammer was merely a poor business adventure by a wealthy firm which should have known better, and which got out of the hole as best it could by having it sold as a gift to the city. Instead of this, the vessel at all times must be pictured as the victim of changing times, the villains of the party being the builders of electrical-driven liners. They are the bad ones.

To board the vessel costs a quarter, but trade

is never good with the possible exception of Sundays. On week days the boy sea scouts are permitted to play around aboard for nothing, the vessel being known as a museum ship. They climb around the rigging and pretend they are putting to sea, but I suspicion that even they at times feel the game is a little forced.

The captain aboard does the best he can for trade. We call him Captain Yumpin Yeesus, derived from his favorite expression, and he can tell some remarkable seagoing yarns to tourists too. Yes, he does his best to promote trade, and yet a sea captain who is always describing how he loves the sea and yet never goes anywhere except uptown to lunch is a little unconvincing. But we reporters never mention that either, for fundamentally we are all a bit amazed at Capt. Yumpin Yeesus for his accomplishments.

If he cannot put to sea under canvas he will not put to sea at all. These are his sentiments, and against them we have no arguments, no proof. We cannot make him demonstrate his words because we all know that this windjammer, having been fast to a pier so long without repairs, would dissolve on hitting the first squall outside. The windjammer simply would disintegrate, and then where would the town's museum ship be, and then where would the captain be, too? It is better just to let things ride as they are and to write the campaign stories with the attitude of spontaneous enthusiasm for anything which has worn a sail.

The captain used to try to talk visitors into coming aboard. He would lean over the side and talk down to sight-seers on the pier, telling them of the vessel's fame. But he does not do that now, even for the sake of the needed funds. He quit this policy all at once. He quit suddenly one Saturday afternoon.

He was giving his customary talk to a man down on the pier, a man who had the appearance of never having left the Dakotas before, and was suggesting that the man come aboard and see what the vessel was like. But the man, after listening awhile, had something to say too. He said: "Why in the name of hell should I pay two-bits to get on that raft when fifteen years ago in Sydney I paid three pounds to get off the dirty pink son-of-a-bitch."

To this the captain had no answer, and the man without another word walked away. But he was not nice, anyway, and only nice customers should board the museum ship now because of the sea scouts being there.

XXI

WE have fish which come ashore here and can be gathered off the beach for eating. But I hesitate to mention them because such phenomena usually occur in the Southern Hemisphere, in the South Seas, in the interior of Africa, far away where only explorers are allowed to report on them.

Yet I do not recall ever having read of similar fish in those countries, and the schoolboy natives there may be interested in learning what is in my own front yard of an ocean. For all of the ocean as far as I can see is my estate, and the vessels moving along the horizon of the estate belong to me, too. They are moving along out there merely for me to watch them.

This also is true of the fish which come ashore on certain nights. On these nights I am a Biblical character. I am living three thousand years ago. The fish are being sent to me as a demonstration that perhaps, after all, there is some sort of God who wants to convert me into a disciple. But the demonstration is not strong enough, and I remain a doubter. Even when the fish shower into the sand by the thousands I still remain a doubter. For the fish may as well come ashore as remain out where they are, and apparently I am hard to please.

These fish are grunion, built much after the order of fair-sized sardines. Grunion belong to the smelt family, yet grunion and smelt are not the same. Unfortunately for the grunion, their arrivals on the beach can be predicted with the accuracy of a time-table. The spring tides, which accompany the full and dark of the moon, are the time-tables by which the grunion runs can be predicted. And unless the grunion watch out they soon may be exterminated as punishment for their own regularity. Nothing on this earth should be as regular as grunion and still hope to survive.

The grunion arrive on the third or fourth nights following the full of the moon and the dark of the moon. For about an hour after the turn of the tide these little fish flop about on the beach. The female digs tail-first into the sand depositing her eggs, which the male fertilizes as he lies arched around her. To be sure, the female makes an undignified show of herself. She spins about on her tail as though indifferent to what other fish may think of her. This is her night, her big minute away from her home the ocean, and she behaves as if drunk. She behaves this way until the figurative stroke of twelve when another wave carries her and her man back to sea where they belong.

The succeeding tides bury the eggs more deeply into the sand where they lie until dug out two weeks later by the next series of high tides. At this time the eggs hatch and the tiny fish are washed into the ocean. Their life has been going on like this for a good many fish-generations now, and their family tree was blackened by the scandal of many beach parties long before the coming of Cabrillo to this sunny coast. But the grunion never will learn to hunt new shorelines distant from the reach of automobiles of this city, and for this reason the grunion-run has turned into an entertainment which I no longer sit up to watch.

On grunion-run night the beach is not the lonely beach of most nights. Instead, the sands are illuminated by fires each few yards. People by the dozens have arrived to turn the ocean, my ocean, into theatricals. And if I had the power to call out to the grunion not to come ashore on these nights I would do so. I would call as loudly as I could. And on some other night when the people were all gone I would whisper to the grunion: "It's all right now. You may come in."

But of course the grunion do arrive, and they arrive on schedule. First a few arrive, and the people begin to scream in their excitement. They have not had fish come right up to them before like this, and in the heat of the chase the people forget about their shoes and their clothing. They follow the fish back into the surf. They capture the fish with their bare hands and with hand-nets and with common window-screen. They jab the screen down into the sand between the grunion and the sea. The ebbing surf rushes through the screen, but the grunion is caught by it and held for capture.

When the run is over, men walk away with grunion by the buckets. And when too many are caught for eating, the surplus is thrown away.

Being the waterfront reporter my job includes writing the story predicting the next grunion runs. But lately I have been growing mighty careless about this assignment. Mighty, mighty careless. The fish-and-game warden knows of my carelessness, but so far he has not told.

XXII

THE harbor master has shown me a new cliff-line up the coast which can be reached only by walking. He originally took me here to fish for lobsters in the pools of the rocky reefs. But since then I have returned so often that this excluded part of the ocean now seems to be mine.

The cliff is about three miles away from the regular highway to the Mexican towns on the border, and the car can be run off into the brush and parked there out of sight. The rest of the journey is made afoot through cacti and prickly brush. Nobody ever tries to make it, as better places along the ocean are more easily reached. Better places where the sand is undisturbed for swimming by these reefs of rock. Volcanic, too, they seem. And porous. And they form lakes and homes for lobsters, ink-fish, eels, for all the creatures which do not spend their days swimming aimlessly.

The most faithful servant of this cliff promenade is the ocean. It cares conscientiously for the long sweep while I am away in town covering the news of the waterfront. The tides are as careful about scrubbing off the sand twice a day as though I had been present watching. For on week-ends the only requirement for making me feel that the earth is dazzling by new and that I am the first man to put foot upon it, is this jagged shoreline when the sand is fresh from an outgoing tide. The reach ahead of me is without a human track, and the only markings are by the minute claws of birds. Not the clumsy markings of sea gulls, for sea gulls make too much noise and are too selfish. But these other tracks are by a tiny bird I cannot name. It may be a small sandpiper, it may be a miniature snipe, but whatever it is it arrives with all its brothers and sisters. They immediately organize themselves into a football team and run signal practice on the glassy surf-line.

The flock swerves as a single bird to right or to left, always in a body and always dependent on the orders of the quarter back. Nor do these birds permit themselves to be bluffed by the surf. If they know where sea food is stored beneath the sand they chase the wave away from it. The birds dig for all they are worth with their beaks until the wave summons enough courage to return. The team retreats a few yards up the sand then, but only for a moment. These birds, traveling with the lightness of the sea foam itself, know they have the ocean's number. And long before now the ocean has given up trying to catch them.

So clean of human footprints is this sand aftei each outgoing tide that even the crabs within the lagoons of the reef have all reason to believe that the entirety of the earth belongs to them. They are startled when I, who am not a crab, come stalking along from out of nowhere. I am a giant who has just arrived from the moon, and the little fellows tumble all over themselves to seek hiding from my course of march. They drop head-first off rocks as high to them as a theatre building. They run for all they are worth for the water or for the coverage of a stone.

On this shoreline of mine, then, I am the conqueror. Nothing can stop me. If no crabs are around to frighten as I walk along I always can resort to pressing my heel upon seaweed bulbs. If the bulbs are fresh they utter an embittered pop against me. But I do not care. I love pops. I love the last outcry of the slain. And I leave my dead lying there on the wet sand of the battlefield. I cannot be bothered burying them. The ocean must attend to such minor details, for I am an important man—on my own shoreline.

Yet in my pursuit of lobsters I must be careful. They are wiser than crabs. They are wiser than seaweed bulbs. They are wiser at times than I. They are not fooled by an hallucination that I have just arrived from another orbit. They know exactly who I am, and they know exactly what I am doing out there on the reef with my long spear. And the only way I can outwit them is by sneaking on them when they are hidden down inside the caves of their deep homes.

The lagoon is sprinkled with tide-swept lakes and lagoons, and down into the most promising of these I lower a breakfast of ancient fishhead. The fishhead is weighted with a stone, the string is long, and all must be performed without a splash. For lobsters of edible size are old fellows. They were not born yesterday. They were born from seven to twelve years ago and they are anxious to have their lives hold many more years for them. They are in no hurry to be boiled alive in a lone shack far beyond hearing of the fish-and-game warden.

If eventually they must be eaten, it seems only natural that they should prefer as the occasion New York with its opening nights and its electric signs that jump. But to be eaten way out West here by a waterfront reporter is a tough break for any lobster, all right, especially if the lobster by waiting awhile might have drawn such men as Broun, Huxley or Hecht. No wonder, then, that the lobsters resist as long as possible the

gaseous odors of my very tempting fishhead.
No wonder the lobsters remain so long inside
their homes without so much as showing an
antenna. They are wise and they are sober and
they are hungry, too. More hungry at times
than wise.

Lying on my stomach above the pool I jar the
fishhead a bit to make more gaseous bubbles roll
from it into the doorway of the lobster's home.
When my dinner guest does decide to experiment
with the meal his motions are as studied and as
timed as those of an actor. The antennae come
into view first. These jointed sticks protrude
ahead. They work with the stiffness of a crane.
They twist to right and to left and upward.
They are so tricky in their motions as to be confused with the long stems of seagrass down
there, for this seagrass waves, too, in keeping
with the under-wash of the ocean.

The lobster knows his act. He is not hasty.
He has only his cleverness for self-protection.
He does not have defending pincers as have his
brothers on the East coast. These lobsters in
the Pacific have only their quickness and their
eyesight. They may be slow about moving forward, but in leaping backward they use the
flipper of their tail as a spring. When they retreat they retreat all at once. They vanish.
They are not there. I must allow for this speed

when I stab with my long spear. I must allow
for the water's refraction too, and I must stab
hard. For their coats are as tough as a little
war tank, and nothing seems to delight them
more than to pretend they are caught and yet
not be caught. Their sense of humor is out-
rageous.

The antennae poke at the fishhead and find it
to be genuine. The head of the lobster follows.
Not much of it, but only an inch or two. This
is enough for a target. It has to be, for the
lobster in the last minute may change its mind
about eating and may dive back, not to re-appear
the rest of the day. I must take my chance, and
I feel the prongs of the spear grasp the armored
coat right around the neck. And there I am with
a lobster and with, I hope, no fish-and-game
Warden watching me from shore. For in these
waters to spear lobsters is contrary to the law.

They may be trapped in season. But I like
lobsters out of season, and to use a trap out of
season might be too conspicuous. For traps a
rowboat would be needed, too. I would need to
row about two miles from shore, then lower the
trap to the bottom of a kelp bed out there. A
hundred or more feet of line would be necessary,
and this is too much line for a reporter to buy.
I would not know what to do with it all after
being retired.

The commercial fishermen catch their lobsters with traps. They are weighted with stones and also carry fishheads as bait. To lower them and to raise them is a hard job, and one time a fisherman's wrist became entangled in the line as he heaved the heavy trap overboard. He was carried to the bottom with it and was drowned, and I shall bring this fact to the attention of the warden should he ever complain of me using a spear. The incident happened five years ago, and if he would not mind waiting a minute before locking me in a cell I could search our old newspaper files for the clipping. I would show it to him and say: "There!"

In this shoreline of mine also can be found an occasional abalone. I would use the plural but it is not given in my dictionary. However, a description of the abalone is given there: "A large gastopod mollusk having a slightly spiral shell, perforated with a row of holes for the escape of water from the gills. The shell is lined with mother of pearl which is used in inlaying, button-making, etc.; an ear shell." The description is easy, but what is hard is freeing the abalone off the deep rocks where they cling. A legal season is on the abalone too, but I must eat, and besides they give me an excuse for swimming during the cold months.

In diving for the abalone is one time I am sure

to wear a swimming suit, in fact two suits to prevent being scratched and also to provide a place for carrying the shells. On releasing them from the rocks on the bottom I stuff the shells between the two suits, and in this way can swim back to shore. Also I wear gloves, for the rocks down there are sharp with barnacles. An abalone is such a big thing, about the size of a bowl, and has such a suction against the rock that a tire-iron is the best thing to use as a pry.

In swimming back to shore with a load of abalone tucked all around me, I appear strangely and cruelly impregnated and beyond all help of a doctor. But the abalone, when finally pounded, sliced and fried, is worth all the mortification of evil rumors. And should the ground squirrels on top the cliff become too fresh with their gossip about me I shall punish them by refusing to give them the empty shells as playthings. I shall throw the shells back into the sea. Or I could take them up to the main highway and sell them to tourists. That is what I could do.

The idea occurred to me just now, just this minute, and shall be held in reserve should an emergency ever arrive with my job on the paper. I can erect a small stand alongside the road, and I can decorate the stand with bunting and with pictures of the presidents and with a loud speaker.

That is the idea and I am a fool not to have thought of the plan before. Because if tourists want anything they want shells, hand-polished shells. They are needed back home for holding doors open and for putting up to the ear like the dictionary explains.

Once a Japanese fisherman dove for an abalone in deep water. He tried to pry the shell free with his bare hands, but his fingers became caught under it. He also was held there until he was drowned just like the lobster fisherman. This happened six years ago, but I tell the story anyway. I tell it whenever I can.

XXIII

OFTEN when men are talking of experiences they have had with wild animals while hunting in the mountains back of here I am tempted to join the conversation by telling of the sea lion I once met while on the beach at night. But the experience, compared to their experiences, was so slight, so absurd, that fortunately I have retained my promise with the sea and with the sea lion and have said nothing out loud to anybody.

At night, of course, when the tide is out the sand of my shoreline becomes snow, ankle-deep. My boots sink into it making the crunch-crunch-crunch sound so familiar in Dakota or Montana during winters. I could be there, and my desolate beach could be a January prairie. For even on the darkest nights, nights when there is no moon and when the stars are blurred, the shoreline maintains that certain radiance so common with snow. This radiance frightens the night away. Night may hover but may not land, and these are the hours to go walking, if walk one will.

I am a fool for these nights, such a fool that I

125

dare tell nobody where I have been. I am too much the coward to be considered by others as erratic, I am deadly afraid of being accused of assuming privileges reserved for geniuses only. During these walks I am treading on territory too sacred for a young man of my sort who in the daytime must earn his living gathering nonsense for my paper. I am walking through a sunken garden where only poets should walk, poets and other people who through necessity need not be up and going again at daybreak, dodging street cars and listening to stories and saying "Yes, sir," all for the sake of my weekend check.

But once I am on the night beach, once I do sneak through the barriers to where I do not belong, the beach refrains from driving me away. The beach permits me to stay providing I do not advertise the secrets of my visit, and providing I do not invite another mortal along too. For another, no matter how close a friend, is sure at some moment to exclaim: "What a perfectly glorious night!" And presto, at this blandishment the perfectness vanishes. There is no perfectness. It has been frightened into hiding, frightened by self-consciousness. For no night, regardless of how perfect, can endure being screeched at by a mortal.

So, as far as concerns these stolen walks, the

best principle I find is to take them and forget about them, to take them again and to forget about them again, although this forgetting is not always easy. It is not easy in the case of the young sea lion which crawled up the sand from the surf and lay beside me.

I was resting near two boulders at the time. I was lying on my back, one hand under my head, the other hand holding a cigarette aloft. I did not hear the sea lion approach, as this sound would be as nothing compared to the sound of the surf. I did not hear the surf either, as I have lived too long by the ocean to be aware of the surf-beat. I do not notice it except during storms or when somebody draws the sound to my attention. My first awareness, then, that something alive was alongside me was when I felt the wet body nosing into my side. I put my hand there quickly, also I jerked my head quickly to look.

The baby sea lion, I believe, was as astonished as I, for its round eyes stared at me for having made such a sudden movement. Obviously the little fellow had come to me for warmth, as I could see now that it had not long been abandoned by its mother. The youngster was probably an orphan, and now that the first surprise of our meeting was over we accepted a sort of working agreement. The seal would not get me all wet if I would not pet it or patronize it too much. "We'll just stay the way we are, eh?" This was our agreement.

An early impulse, naturally, was to make a captive of the seal, to take it back to the city as proof somewhat of my story. The impulse was the same, perhaps, which drives men to lug home heads of deer to demonstrate a hidden valiance. Yet the more I studied my little companion the more I felt like laughing at the idiocy of the impulse. Canaries must be caged. Deer must be beheaded. Dogs must be turned into pampered dolls of sawdust. And coyotes, because they refuse to wear a collar and a license, must be shot.

The hair began to dry now. It became dry and soft between my fingers. We lay there for an hour or more, but because I would have to be at work in the morning I could not lie there forever. So, looking at the small creature, I all but said aloud: "You're a silly little beast to have come up here beside me. Don't you know there's a bounty of five dollars on your scalp? Your ma or your old man should have told you something about us. Listen, I'm going to let you go back into the water, and don't ever let me catch you doing this again."

As I arose, the youngster's tremendously round eyes watched me trudge away, yet he did not move from the warm spot we had created. I glanced back over my shoulder and could see the head silhouetted upwards watching me. Whether he accepted my advice I have no way of knowing. But I do know I have walked this same lonely stretch many times since then, and no young sea lion, nothing alive whatsoever on the snow-sand.

XXIV

THE new fish-and-game investigator came up to the office and said that too many people along the shoreline were catching lobsters out of season and that he needed two more deputies to help put a stop to the law-breaking.

He wanted the city editor's support to obtain these deputies, and said that almost any night people drive their cars to the coastline in deserted places, and there drop their lobster hoop-nets at high tide off the rocks.

He could cruise the coastline in his own launch, he said, but he needed more deputies to work from the shore-side. He said he would like to prove to the city editor how bad the situation really was, and he suggested that I go with him on a night's patrol duty.

"All right," the city editor nodded to me. "You go with him if he wants you to." I went with him, and he put me ashore on a peninsula about nine miles from the city.

"Here's where fishermen come almost every night, I'm told," he advised me. "And you'll see how many nets they have. I'll go on with the rest of the patrolling and call back for you."

He chugged his launch back out to sea. He was looking for rowboat-poachers who dropped their traps offshore by the kelp beds, and as soon as he left I made myself at home far out on the rocky point. I who poach more than most poachers did not like this new role of mine, and certainly had no notion to strain myself in trying to be conscientious.

With a rock for a seat and another rock for a back I broke out my cigarettes to complete my comfort. Fishermen might see the red tips, but I did not care. I was not hiding. The moon was three-quarters, which is almost as bright as a full moon, and I could make out the country as plainly as though the time was dawn instead of ten at night.

Within a half-hour the first headlights appeared on the little dirt road to the peninsula. A grove of gum trees is there, forming a natural three-sided wall around the place. The open side was towards the sea and towards me, and the car drove within the shelter and stopped. The lights went out, first the headlights, then the parking lights, and the car had a sharper outline with the lights off than on.

The shadows in the car sat there awhile, between the moon and me. They had been cut out of pasteboard in a kindergarten, and finally the shadow behind the steering wheel bent towards the shadow on the right, making one shadow.

And this one shadow gradually sank beneath the horizon of the car, and I knew by then that these shadows had brought no lobster traps. These shadows were eliminated, so I turned to sea watching for the return of the investigator.

In time the car's headlights were turned on again, filling this deserted world with a blinding yellow. The motor started, the car backed around and was gone over the same narrow road back to the main highway, the ancient surf retaining its ancient rhythm as though nothing at all had happened. And surprisingly soon another pair of headlights felt their way along the curves of the dirt road. This second car drove to within the same clearing between the gum trees and the point, and again the lights were extinguished, and again the pasteboard shadow behind the steering wheel bent towards the shadow on the right, making one shadow, this one shadow again sinking below the car's horizon. No lobster fishermen this time, either, so I lit a new cigarette, hoping the shadows would know I was down on the rocks if they wanted to know I was down on the rocks.

After the second car left a third car arrived, and it was as if there had not been three cars, but that the same car had arrived each time, so exact was the repetition of the shadow ritual, with such monotonous perfection did the new shadows imitate the shadows which had gone on before. As at the pull of the same string these new pasteboards performed with the same mechanical surety of the previous pasteboards, and I knew now that I had observed, not the shadows of individuals, but the shadows of generations. I was not a human now, but was detached from the animal kingdom. I was some idol without breath of my own or flesh of my own, but only with sight and eternity and with an odd sort of interest in the machinery of these things called the living. Generation had followed generation to this secluded peninsula, each generation had danced its dance, had implanted the kernel of itself, and had departed, had vanished with old age, back into the void of the main highway. Each car was sixty years or seventy years, and only I on the rocks was deathless, only I on the rocks was permitted to count by centuries where these three generations had counted by summers.

The investigator's launch drew alongside now and I sprang aboard directly from the rocks, so calm was the sea that night. I did not have to wade, the ocean was like a lake. And when he asked me if I had seen anything I had to answer him, of course, that I had seen nothing, as I had no way of conveying to him that what I had seen were two hundred years.

"That's funny," he said. "That's damn funny. People say there's fishermen driving out here 'most every night."

XXV

NOT far from here is San Nicolas island which some day I shall put into writing. We all have a place we are some day going to put into writing, and this is mine, and I have been preparing now for a number of years.

This is the reason when an author comes to town I try to manage to be assigned to interview him. If he arrives by liner I have no difficulty obtaining the assignment, but frequently he arrives by train. Then I have to obtain permission to leave the waterfront and interview him in his hotel.

I say to the author: "There's an interesting island around here I'm going to write up some day myself."

He replies: "So?"

I reply: "Yes."

He replies: "I understand you don't have much rain down in this section of the country."

I reply: "On certain days when there's a mirage you can almost see the island from this hotel." I step to the west window and look, but as usual the First National Bank building is there.

"No," I apologize. "You can't see it from here on account of a building."

"That certainly is too bad. It certainly is, now. How long about does it take to reach Tijuana from here? Or Agua Caliente?"

"Not very long if you're driving."

"Well, I hardly intended to walk exactly. How long by auto?"

"Not very long. But on this island was the Lost Woman. She lived on it alone for eighteen years. They tried to find her and bring her off, but she always ran away and hid. She was an Indian. Don't you think it would make a story, all right?"

"Undoubtedly. Undoubtedly. It is as interesting as can be."

"She was an Indian. She lived on it alone for eighteen years. She could have gotten off, but she always ran and hid. How would you handle it, do you think?"

"I really hardly know, I'm sure."

"But if you did know, how would you handle it, do you think? You see, this was a long time ago. Do you want to know the location of the island?"

"Yes. Why, yes, indeed."

"It's one of the Channel Islands group. Do you want me to show it to you on the map?"

"Yes. Why, yes, indeed."

"Have you a map?"

"No."

"Well, if you had a map it would be right over here. See. My finger is the mainland. And right over here by my thumb, this thumb that's moving, that's San Nicolas. Fishermen went over from here to get her a lot of times, but they could never find her. They think she ran into a cave. The island has lots of caves down along the shoreline."

"Caves are always interesting, to be sure."

"Yes, they are. Russian otter hunters one time lived on the island for two years. They killed off the men Indians and kept the women. Would that be too risqué, do you think?"

"No, I guess not."

"No, I guess not, either. It would have been too risqué a few years ago maybe, though, don't you think?"

"If I started for Agua Caliente right now could I be back in time for my lecture at eight?"

"Perhaps. Yes, I believe you could. You see, the Russians left after a while. The women were left on the island all alone. The Isle of Women. Missionaries heard about them and sent over a small vessel to get them. The women were rounded up and taken aboard. They could not speak English very well, and just as the anchor was being weighed one of the women made a scene. She saw she was being taken away, and she had left her baby ashore. She leaped overboard and swam to the beach. A storm was coming up and the captain dare not fool around the breaker-line any longer. He had to clear out and leave her there. She lived on fish and mussels and she dressed herself in sealskins and sea-gull feathers. Just imagine."

"Just imagine."

"As years went by she grew frightened of people. Fishermen knew she was on there and frequently while fishing near by they went ashore out of curiosity. But they could not find her. But .eighteen years later an expedition larger than the others landed on the island to make a thorough search for her. Although it searched the island from end to end it could not find her either. Can you beat it?"

"No."

"The expedition returned three times without success, but on the fourth time—"

"It found her."

"Yes. One of the men saw her on an opposite hill. The sun was in her eyes and she was skinning a seal to make a—"

"Dress."

"Yes. She did not see the man because of the sun in her eyes, and he sneaked up to her. He was afraid she would bite or scratch. But when she saw she was captured she surrendered like a sport. She handed him a hunk of the raw seal to eat. Wouldn't that make a story?"

"A wonderful, wonderful story. What's the time?"

"About 1850 or '51. I'll look and make sure."

"Yes, look and make sure."

XXVI

AMONG my souvenirs, such as the fan letter I once received and such as the newspaper picture of the back of my head in a group interviewing two endurance flyers, I also have a third souvenir. It is a swordfish sword.

This souvenir is in memory of the day I went swordfishing with Mello aboard his swordfish-boat *Genoa*. He makes his living catching swordfish. He harpoons them, and his craft is rigged with a boom far out over the bow.

Swordfish have to be approached with care. They will dive at the least sound of a motor. They will dive, too, if crossed by the shadow of a boat. Passengers aboard a liner never see swordfish, for the liner makes too much noise. But off the coast here is a patch of water about twenty miles square where the swordfish come to the surface to bask in the sun.

A man like Mello does not have to catch more than one swordfish a day to make a living, these fish averaging well over a quarter-ton and bringing fifteen to thirty dollars each. From this must come the cost of the gasoline and the wages of an assistant. For two men really should work on the job. Mello brought along his other man the day I went with him, as I apparently did not count.

Mello prefers a glassy sea and the noon sun. He thinks more swordfish rise to the surface at noon than at any other time. He stands on top the pilot house watching for their tails or fins. He says that the broadbill, the marlin and the Japanese swordfish each has a different way of lying on the surface. He can tell by the tail or the fin just which variety he has sighted, and he has a different method for approaching each.

His eyesight means everything to him, and every night he bathes his eyes in a solution. He confided this to me if I would promise not to tell other swordfish men. But other swordfish men secretly bathe their eyes too. Whether this bathing does any good I do not know, but the competition among the men is as strong as among boxers. Each man wants to be the champion for the season, and Mello has been champion twice in succession.

He has been after swordfish for so many years that he knows all about them, when they arrive here out of nowhere and when they are most likely to disappear till next season. He said he has seen fights between a swordfish and a shark, and he intimated that the fights were pretty bad. The shark, sneaking up from behind, lunges for the swordfish's tail, and if the tail is caught the fight is over. For the swordfish then has no way of steering itself around for an attack. But if the shark misses, the swordfish leaps from the water and zooms down at the shark and usually hits with its sword. Sometimes two or more sharks attack at once, and that is rather bad too.

As much as I wanted a sword of my own as a curio I did not want the sword unless I myself harpooned the fish. Mello and I, shouting back and forth between the deck and the pilot house, made an agreement. He would let me try my luck with the harpoon on a wager. If I missed I was to pay him fifteen dollars, the minimum loss of the catch. But if I did not miss he not only was to give me the sword but also would polish and cure it for me. This seemed fair enough and we sighted the stick of our first swordfish at noon, as he said we would.

He called directions down the speaking tube to the man at the wheel. The *Genoa* circled sharply to port and approached the stick from the rear. To try to close in on the fish from the side does little good, for the large eyes have a clear vision on each side and the fish will dive on the least suspicion. Mello ordered the motors shut off, and he leaped from the pilot house to

the forward deck.   He hurried out to the end of
the boom.   The harpoon, twice his own length,
was ready and waiting for him out there.

The *Genoa* coasted the remaining few yards
without a sound.   Mello grasped the harpoon
and with all the strength of his shoulders he
buried the harpoon deeply into the fish before it
had time to know he was anywhere around.   The
fish, surprised and dragging fathoms of line behind it, sounded for the bottom.   There it lay
wondering what had happened to it.

Mello was as excited as though this had been
the first catch of his life.   The harpoon handle,
attached to another line, was let to drop from
his hands over the side to be hauled aboard later.
He rushed back along the boom to the deck and
was too excited to speak or to notice us.

I asked the man at the wheel: "Does he always
get this way?"

"Always.   Except he gets worser as he goes
along.   Damn me if he doesn't."

Mello was now on the aft deck making two
oil cans fast to the end of the harpoon line.
These empty cans would serve as surface
markers until we could return and haul the fish
aboard.   It would be well spent by that time and
should not cause trouble.   For sometimes a
swordfish, if hauled up too soon, is filled with
fight.   Once in these waters a wounded sword-

fish stabbed its sword through the bottom of the boat and became stuck there. The fisherman, afraid the fish would whip around until the boat was capsized, cut off the end of the sword with a hatchet. He used the chopped-off end to plug the hole. He had to work fast as the sea was pouring through. But this fisherman was not Mello. For Mello never hauls his catch up too soon. He leaves it spend itself on the bottom while he continues searching for more sticks during the magical hour of noon. He does not like to waste time. We left the two empty cans floating in the sun astern of us, and were on our way.

"All right," Mello nodded. "The next'll be yours. Do it like I did it. Better get out on the boom now." He replaced another head onto the harpoon handle and handed the gear over to me. Standing out by myself on the end of the boom I felt both proud and a little silly.

We must have cruised for ten or fifteen minutes when he called to the man at the helm: "Hard to port, Madruga."

The *Genoa* swerved to port and Mello called softly out to me: "Don't get excited. Don't get excited."

I was not excited. I was nervous, but not excited. Mello himself was the one who was excited. For if I missed I would miss, and that

is all there would be to it. I was not performing
before a world's series bleachers. I was way out
in the ocean quite by myself.

But he called to me again: "Don't get excited.
Don't get excited." I was tempted to answer
him over my shoulder, but by now I could see
the swordfish ahead of me and it needed all my
attention. I poised my harpoon. The engine
stopped. We were coasting in silence for the
final plunge.

Yet before I could do anything, Mello was out
on the boom beside me. He had leaped off the
top of the pilot house, and had hurried out the
boom as fast as he could. Too excited to speak,
he crowded the harpoon from my hands and
motioned me to return to deck.

My back was turned on him when he stabbed
the harpoon, for as yet I had not quite reached
the deck, and besides I was rather annoyed.
The man at the wheel saw the way I was feeling.
He smiled: "Cheer up. He always does that."

"Why, has he made the same promise to you,
Madruga?"

"Ever' time I go out. An' I been going out
with him three years."

Mello had made his catch, all right, the second
of the day. He was on the aft-deck now making fast two more empty oil cans. He must
have felt me staring at him, for when he

glanced up from his lines he appeared painfully embarrassed.

"I'm sorry," he apologized. "Damn but I'm sorry."

"You can't help harpooning them all yourself, can you, Mello?"

"I guess that's it," he admitted. "I guess that's just it."

He did, though, scrape and polish the sword for me. But if anybody asks me if I made the catch myself I shall have to manage somehow to talk about other things.

XXVII

THE Apollo family is too heathen to live in the fishermen's colony. Mr. Apollo has his own home a few miles up the coastline beyond the city limits. He goes directly there at the conclusion of each cruise, his job being skipper of the small motorboat which runs between here and Mexico.

He does not believe in the divinity of Jesus or in the personality of God or in the sacredness of Sundays, and his vessel has no chapel. When a boy in the old country his parents made him sing in the boys' church choir, and they told him so much about hell that he used to lie awake nights wondering how he possibly would be able to endure having his feet being charred constantly. He used to touch matches to his thumb hoping to see if in time he could make himself accustomed to fire. He never has forgiven his parents for what they told him, nor does he hold their memory dear. He is a heathen in another way, too. This is around his home.

He has no domestic plants growing near his home, but only wild ones. Fundamentally they perhaps are weeds, yet with the respect he gives them they assume a sort of arrogance, a sort of confidence in themselves that at the next turn of the hat they will not be torn up to give their tiny space on this earth to a pampered marigold. The flowered weeds which come to his home have a chance to survive during their few months here on the world, and in appreciation they seem to do the best they can for him.

His one regret is that the drouth of this country prohibits his yard from having a natural spring. But he fudged on Nature by building a spring of his own with second-hand piping. The piping, all hidden under dirt, leads away from the house and up a hill of rock. There high on the rocks the water bubbles slowly up to the surface as though the spring were natural. He has the whole ocean to play with, yet for meditative pleasure he prefers watching this thread of water trickling down from one ridge of rocks to the next. This trickle has more significance to him than has Niagara, and apparently more significance to his children too, of which he has five.

He has permitted Satan to enter their bodies as well as his own. Their house is so isolated from other houses that the youngsters for the most part wear only garauches to protect their feet from the pincushion cacti of the yard. Apollo says they can stay naked as long as they want to stay naked. He says he still has a horror of his own robes which pinned up the back.   But the heathen in him is not limited to his actions.   There is a heathen bluntness to his tongue too, as well I remember from the time I once drove him home from the waterfront.

He had just returned from a two-months' cruise.   He had struck bad weather and had to remain under the cover of Turtle Bay.   But now that he finally was back he wanted to reach his home right away.   He did not want to wait for the stage, so he asked if I would mind driving him there.

I drove him into his dooryard and he told me not to go as he wanted me to stay for lunch. "But," he added, "I hope you'll not mind waiting a minute till I say hello to my wife."

He met her in the doorway just as she was rushing outside to meet him, but before she could say a word he hoisted her completely up from the porch and carried her, laughing, back through the doorway, and the door closed behind them.

All of twenty minutes passed before they reappeared.   She was wearing a different frock and her face was as fresh as a girl's.   His own face, too, was rejoicingly erased of his two months at sea.   He waved happily to me, and the heathen in him said: "You can come in now. I just wanted to make sure first that my wife would keep her mind on the cooking."

XXVIII

SOME charitable organization should find a method whereby I could distribute to all poor little boys and girls the gift which is always coming my way. Other reporters are constantly telling me of the presents they receive, presents such as pipes, hats, quart bottles and cartons of cigarettes. Yet these are as nothing compared to what is offered me—plane rides.

Something about my face must invite this gift, for the situation has gone so far now that were all the invitations accepted as fast as they arrive my typewriter may as well be hung in the sky somewhere and all my waterfront notes written while I am riding around.

Each manager of each local flying field (and the city is famous for having no dearth of them) has received the impression that because I am titled the aviation reporter I must be interested in aviation. The title was handed to me because no paper is complete without it. I am the waterfront reporter on all days except when air caravans come to town or when the Navy or Army is pulling an aerial maneuver. Then I automatically become the aviation reporter until the caravans leave again or until the military planes land. The same thing happens when women flyers come here, or when some more of the boys go aloft for another endurance flight. The whole reason is because the fields happen to be near the bay. I should complain, but would not know what words to use against such positive reasoning. And besides, the time is now too late. The time was too late six years ago.

"We've a new ship," the commercial managers say to me. "How about going up in her and giving us a story." I have looked down on the top of this city so many times that it is nothing more now than a last year's calendar map still hanging on the wall. I am as weary of the sight of goggles and helmets as I am weary of the sight of the Chamber of Commerce shaking hands in front of a plane. Whose plane? Anybody's plane.

The situation would be different if the Lord had anointed me to be one of His children pioneers of the air. But He did not do it. In fact He did not even mention it. I care little about aviation. I have seen too much of it and have written too much about it. I become airsick and all that sort of thing, and yet have been pulled by propellers across the continent both ways, north and south, east and west. I cannot make it all out, for I hardly asked for the rides. The country when seen from the top bores me. I may as well be looking at the rough plastering on the wall. Yet presumably hundreds of chaps would chew up their grandmothers for the very aerial opportunities I try to dodge.

I did not want to be a flyer. What I wanted to be is a great novelist. And yet no publishers ever come around begging me to write, like these field managers come around begging me to ride. No, the publishers do not even come around. I never see them. I see new ships instead. And rather than be asked to write a new serial I am invited to write about tail-skids and wing-angles. I think there must be something dirty about it all. For these flyers do not care about literature. And yet they are asked not only to write books but also to write for *The Saturday Evening Post,* and when I see My Maker this is the first thing I am going to demand of Him, an explanation. I am pretty angry, and if the explanation is not satisfactory I may right up and walk out on Him.

I have had no special desire to become an intimate friend of celebrated pilots. Whom I wanted to meet was Dorothy Parker and Dreiser and Ruth Suckow and the Beards. I wanted to have folks like them dropping in on me on Saturday nights for beer and crackers. Instead, the writers I know are virtually none, but the pilots I know form a list as long as from my knees to my chin. As a result I wonder how many more mountains I will have to look down upon and how many more of Nature's grandeurs, and I wonder how many more motors I will have to sit hour after hour watching from in back. I do not know and I do not care. I used to care, but not any more. For I have decided to go at the thing from a new angle now. I have decided to pretend that I want to be a famous flyer the worst way in the world. This attitude, I hope, may reverse the situation and may cause publishers instead of field managers to phone me saying: "We've a great idea for your new book. How about coming out here to our field and giving it a try."

And I will answer: "Pooh.   Flying's my game."

XXIX

THIS morning a girl I had known in university entered the editorial rooms. Her hair was black, her eyes were black, and she still retained the staunch appearance of the great unlicked.

She did not see me immediately, for my typewriter is hidden by a pillar. This permitted me time to sneak into my coat and to pull my tie tight against my collar. For I have reached that don't-care stage of life now where the knot of my tie droops until the button of my collar peeks its head up over the top. I used to try to break my tie of this habit, but have given up except when going out at nights.

"Hello." This was her voice and she was walking straight towards me. Women as a rule do not interrupt work around our office, for they constantly are entering and leaving. They either are advertising women or they come upstairs to see the society editor or they are wives arriving on pay day. But this girl was such a contrast to the home product of our little city that the boys unconsciously delayed the work they were doing. Perhaps they did not realize they were staring so hard, but I had no way of telling them.

Like a galley slave arising from the thwarts I arose from my tiny lopsided desk and said to her: "My good gosh." And before she could have anything to say in the matter I pushed her on out of the office ahead of me. I virtually shooed her out, and down on the street I pushed her into my coupe which runs on company's gas.

"Listen, why did you come?"

She replied that she had no real reason for coming, except out of curiosity. She said she was passing through town and had stopped off to see how many children I had.

"Your count's as good as mine. Just press that cigarette-holder and they'll all drop out."

"Then you're not married yet?"

"No, but I've a sort of office of my own down on the harbor." I tried to recall other accomplishments and other possessions to describe to her, but this one item marked the beginning and the ending of my list, the alpha and the omega, as we used to sing in Sunday School. We drove on, my car automatically heading for the waterfront like an old horse accustomed only to its ancient delivery route. To have turned in another direction would have hurt the horse's feelings.

"Where we going?" she asked.

"I wanted to show you the harbor."

"I'm not interested in harbors. All I want is to know more about you."

"But my life is so involved. Be more specific."

"Maybe that's right," she smiled. "Yet honestly now, you must like it down here. You've stayed so long."

"It's the money I'm after. And where've you been?"

"In San Francisco. In Detroit. In Chicago. And a short while in New York."

"My gosh, what are you selling?"

"Myself. Look me over."

"That's all I have been doing," I admitted.

"Listen. In all seriousness for a change, what do you do on the paper? Are you the editor?"

"Me? I'm the best waterfront reporter in town. See those fishboats out there. I write about them. See that dredger. Well, I write about it. I tell how much dirt it takes up each month for a turning-basin. See those two piers. Well, we're going to have another just like them. Yes, we are. The bonds already have been voted."

"No, all joking aside. What do you do? Are you the editor?"

"No, I'm not the editor."

"Then what are you really? Tell me."

"I've told you. I said I write about turning-basins, fish, dredgers, dirt and things."

Her answer this time was a softly spoken "oh." And, although she remained in the city until train-time that evening, we somehow never got around to getting married.

XXX

CHARLIE RYAN, who charters his shoreboat to fishing parties, has built a fishpool of his own in his backyard, and that is just one more of the things I do not understand about him.

He said he built the fishpool for his little girl, which is true enough. But he hangs around the rim more than she does, although after all these years of going to sea for fish I should think that by now he would be pretty sick of looking at any more.

But he built the pool all in one night. His little girl had been to a party where there was a fishpool in the patio. On returning home she told her father all about it and asked him for one. He said: "All right, then." He just had time to reach the lumber yard before it closed, and he bought two sacks of cement and seven sacks of sand. He dug for two hours making the pit, and the rest of the night he spent mixing the cement and plastering it over the sides and the bottom, three inches thick. He cemented a yard of pipe through the side for a drain, and when morning came there was the fishpool. He

161

said he was almost as surprised as anybody to see it there.

Later he put in a lot of large stones, making tunnels and caves underwater, and he put in some water lilies, the kind which float around on bulbs and do not need to be planted on the bottom in cans.

When he took me to his home to look at the pool I at first protested about going. I am not interested in fishpools or in fish either, and told him so. But he answered that I would be interested in these. He said they were not the ordinary kind. But what he really meant, I discovered, was that they were so ordinary as to be unordinary. They were not goldfish. They were trout, ordinary trout. And I am sure that if the pond had been filled with salt water instead of fresh water he would have had everyday mackerel inside there, the same kind which sports fishermen do not bother bringing home, but throw back into the ocean dead.

"But, Charlie, what's the idea? People don't keep trout in pools as fancy as this."

He explained that he had intended to be practical, that he would like fresh-water fish around whenever he wanted them as a change to what he caught at sea. He wanted fresh trout as a surprise whenever he had company.

"I'm company," I smiled, not expecting him to answer me seriously.

"No, I'm not ready to eat them yet. Maybe later. We've talked it over."

"Who's talked it over?"

"That's just a joke. I meant the fish and me. Listen." He knelt down at the pool so closely that his chin almost rested on one of the stones. Two of the four trout stared out at him from beneath a cave. Their tails waved slowly behind them and they exchanged looks with him look for look.

"Am I to be eaten today, Charlie?" said Charlie in a diminutive and twisted tone.

"No, not today," said Charlie to the fish.

"Thank you, Charlie. But how about to-morrow?"

"Well, that's something else again. We'll see how you behave."

"We'll behave all right." That tiny tone again.

"Then see that you do."

"We'll see. And thank you. Thank you very much. And maybe the day after the day after tomorrow you'll not eat us either. What do you think?"

"I think the four of you are trying to get promises from me you don't deserve. You're trying to work me, but we'll see."

With that he arose, grinned, and studied me: "Damn it all, but do you know I get a lot of fun being silly around them like that."

"Not silly at all." For I could see he was embarrassed. "There's sometimes a lot of fun in things besides eating them."

"No, I think my mind's finally on the skids. Too much fishing. It gets us all in time, you know. Yet it seems odd as hell that this is the first time I ever paid attention to fish. They've always been just slabs of wood to me. No nerves, no desire to live, no nothing. Just food floating around the same as apples grow on trees."

This simile, I admit, puzzled me, as never before had I ever heard fish described as apples on trees. We walked away from the pool, then, and went inside the house for a pitcher of Dago red. I did think, though, that I understood what he had in mind. For often I, too, have been astonished at the indifference with which the lives of fish are handled, no romance whatsoever being attached to their suffocating deaths. But this was the first time, the very first time, I ever had seen an inkling of a similar opinion in another. I never have had the nerve to express my own fleet thought out loud as it made me feel a bit foolish, even thinking of it to myself.

But on fishermen's wharf day after day I see the fish, stiff with ice, hauled aloft and loaded into hand trucks for the wholesale markets across the street. And at the canneries the same thing happens, only there the fish are placed on endless chains for the last ride. 'And dead fish do have expressions. This expression is frozen right into them, for so quickly are they alive one moment and in ice the next. They do have expressions, an expression of immense and sudden suffering, and an expression of surprise, too, all frozen in the eye. But so many of them are killed at once that, like soldiers left on a battlefield, they could not possibly have suffered individual pain, and I feel sheepish even to have given it a moment's thought.

But still the eye of a fish is a beautiful thing, yet to say so would produce only laughter, although nobody of my acquaintance could make one. And so I know at times that I am a bit off, all right, and poor Charlie must have felt he was becoming the same way, neither of us understanding how a person who would be indifferent to a pack could become attached to individuals segregated from the pack. He did not understand either, apparently, because after awhile he returned to the front room from the kitchen. He asked me to stay for supper. He urged me to stay. And as though to redeem himself for his afternoon's display of weakness we had fish. Without my knowing what he was doing he had asked his wife to prepare them. And there they were on the table, the four trout, one for him, one for his wife, one for his little girl, and an extra one for whoever wanted it.

XXXI

SOMEDAY something would happen to the liner, we all knew, because she was so regular. Such regularity as hers did not belong to the sea. Her regularity belonged to trains or to subways, but not to tides and currents, wind and fog.

The liner arrived at eight in the evening and departed at nine in the morning. Twice a week the vessel did this, twice a week for ten years, five months and four days. Then it happened, and now the double bottom of the liner is held by sharp rocks and a shoal of sand. Before daylight this morning the liner cut too close to shore in a fog. Not a heavy fog, but enough to hide the lighthouse on the point.

All day I have been working on the story. The Navy radio operator telephoned me at five.

"You better get to your office," he said. "You might want to put out an extra."

I waited for him to explain, but a little of the actor is in him and he was waiting for the proper suspense. He was waiting for me to ask what had happened, and this I did ask.

He told me then, quickly, all he knew. I

hurried and dressed, and as I dressed, the newspaper-mania in me said: "What a story." And another part of me said: "It isn't true, of course."

Even after all these months of expecting the thing would happen, the actuality was too surprising to believe. For this liner was no ordinary coastal liner. Her sides were of such clean white that they dazzle when struck by the sun. The liner has operated out of here for so long that it is part of the harbor, the same as the sand bar, the same as the channel beacons.

The liner itself will not really be missed until next week. We will start to miss the vessel then, for its familiar berth on the south side of the main pier will be vacant. On Tuesdays and Fridays we will look for the liner, but it will not be there.

The vessel belonged to the Navy for awhile and had for mascots a cat and a monkey. The two would have gotten along all right together except for the monkey. It would wait until the cat was asleep on deck, then the monkey would sneak up and with its tail grab the tail of the cat. Dragging the cat backwards along the deck, the monkey would gallop as fast as possible forward and aft. Sparks would fly from the cat's claws whenever they crossed steel, and whoever was around would try to put a stop to the affair. But the monkey was too fast, and would not release the cat until near a ladder. Then the monkey would let go and scamper up into the rigging.

The cat, its dignity hurt beyond words, would sit below the rigging and wait for the monkey to come down, which the monkey would not do. That is, until after the cat pretended to go off into hiding. Then the monkey would screech a tremendous screech and dash down to within a yard of the deck, but no further. For as sure as anything there would be the cat waiting. It had leaped out from its hiding, as the monkey knew the cat would do.

This game would last to unendurable lengths. But once the cat did not dash out from hiding. And the monkey, bewildered at the absence, dared for once to come all the way down on deck. The cat, coming from nowhere, dove at the monkey then and would have caught it, but the monkey leaped down a hatch into the engine room.

The monkey was not used to the engine room and was frightened of the moving crankshaft and flywheel, and ran into a cubbyhole and hid. For two days and two nights the monkey hid there without food or water, and did not come out until the vessel reached port and the engines were brought to a stop. This was the cat's revenge, though whether it was fully satisfied none of us know.

Until today I almost had forgotten this

incident. But in doing the rush work on the wreck I was amazed how often the episode of the cat and the monkey returned to me, though of course I could not use the episode in my news copy. The old affairs between a cat and a monkey do not insert themselves well into a story involving the rescue of five hundred passengers, or to be exact, four hundred and ninety-six passengers. But the history of the liner (and the history I had to write today too) is hardly complete without the two unfriendly companions. I must record them somewhere, if merely for myself like this.

XXXII

THE shoreboat from which we distributed Johnny Lafferty's ashes is No. 34. He owned the boat. His wife thought nothing would be more appropriate, then, than to have the ashes distributed to sea from there.

She made an occasion of it, for the shoreboat is large, almost as large as a cruiser. Enough room was aboard for members of the women's auxiliary of his lodge, and also for as many men members of the lodge as could get away in the morning.

"You were quite a friend of John's," she said to me. "Why don't you come along and write it up for the paper." I tried to get out of it, as the affair was hardly news, and the trip outside and back would take two hours. But Mrs. Lafferty is Mrs. Lafferty, and with her the best way is to accept with eagerness and to hope to get out of it later by having something unavoidable happen, such as a ship explosion. For Mrs. Lafferty is a woman about whom may be used the word "determined."

She is broad-shouldered and has the gait of a man. She married Johnny five years ago when he was only a lobster-fisherman. She made him what he was. She brought him in from the sea and had him trade his lobster-boat for shore-boat No. 34. In this he carried passengers for awhile out to the warships. But Mrs. Lafferty still was not satisfied. She had him change his fisherman's clothes for a white uniform and a white cap, and she had shoreboat No. 34 refitted into an excursion boat for taking tourists around the bay.

Johnny in his white suit would stand at the wheel and answer their questions. He would describe the harbor's "principal points of interest," and usually Mrs. Lafferty would make the sight-seeing trips with him to see that he was speaking his pieces rightly. She had him join a lodge too, for she was a hard worker and believed in causes and fellowship.

In place of an ordinary canvas top she had the excursion boat decked with a striped awning trimmed with tassels. It was quite conspicuous and quite gay, and whatever objections Johnny may have had to his new life he concealed pretty well from us. This perhaps was wise of him, for Mrs. Lafferty is not much given to being contradicted.

"Oh, Johnny," we would say, when she was not around. "Don't forget it's lodge-meeting night tonight." Or sometimes we would address him as Captain Lafferty because of the brass lettering she had placed on his cap.

And then one morning he was found stiff and smiling in his tiny engine room forward. He had died of fume-poisoning, supposedly while preparing the motor. But the forward portholes were closed and so was the hatch from the inside, closed and fastened with a hook. A monkey wrench was in his hand, he was curled over the flywheel as though working, and because of these facts the coroner gave him the benefit of the doubt.

Mrs. Lafferty arranged the funeral, first the cremation, then the scattering of the ashes at sea. That his ashes be scattered on the sea, the same sea which he had deserted, was at his own written request. And Mrs. Lafferty graciously conceded him the favor.

She asked me to bring a news photographer on the trip, but to this I had to draw the line. The story was not worth it, and so I had to tell her that all the photographers were busy at a trial in the courthouse. She did not believe me, of course, but a commercial photographer did come along, one she hired herself.

When shoreboat No. 34 reached a point several miles beyond the bar, the engine was stopped. The photographer set up his camera, and Mrs. Lafferty with the small urn of ashes took her position on the starboard. Somebody dared tell her that a widow really should let others attend to the actual scattering.

"I was his wife," she answered with a tone to which there could be no reply.

The camera was ready, so was she. But meanwhile the boat, not being under headway, had swung around a little with the wind. Both the pilot and I wanted to shout to her to get on the leeward. We started to shout, but knowing her the way we did, we held our voices. She flung the ashes as though they were grass seed, and like grass seed they were blown back into the boat, and poor Johnny Lafferty went over everybody.

During the awful silence on the way back to port the pilot whispered to me: "She messed him up even to the very end, didn't she?"

But Mrs. Lafferty had her own interpretation. Cornering me before we reached the pier she said: "Now, there's a point you can use in your article, young man. How right up to the last minute John didn't want to leave the boat he loved so well."

XXXIII

MIKE BACHALACHI died on a busy day, or he might have made a feature story. The next day was busy too, and the third day is rather too late to do a feature story on anybody who dies around the waterfront.

But this morning I saw the bait-boat which he had built and of which he was so proud, and that is why I remembered him of a year or so back. For Bachalachi could spot sardine schools in daylight as well as at night, which of course is very unusual and which was responsible for him always being assured of a season's job on the live-bait boat which catches for the sporting barge.

Bachalachi was needed during fishing season and he had no idea how needed he really was or he might have charged more for his services. He has caught sardine schools right inside the bay, which is unusual too, and once he herded a school into the ferry slip. He corralled his net around the fish there, and the ferry had to wait outside the slip until he finished taking them aboard. The passengers did not seem to mind, for they watched him at work. This was about the only time anybody ever watched him at work who were not with the live-bait boat crew.

There must be such a thing as instinct, all right, for he could guide the captain at the most ungodly hours to sardine schools. And I have known him to lie flat down on the forward deck and cock his ear over the bow. He said he was listening for sardines, a new stunt we had not heard of before. He originated the idea and he alone could do it. On days when the sea was of steel-plating, so calm, he would signal the captain to shut off the engine. Bachalachi would lie on his stomach then and listen down into the water. He said that the sardines make a funny little noise as they flip their tails and that he could hear them. None of the rest of us could, but he was not lying, for in emergencies he did locate schools in the daytime this way instead of waiting for moonless nights, and the sporting fishermen out on the deep-sea barge had him to thank many times for saving their Sundays. He would bring live bait when nobody else could, and then he announced he was building a live-bait boat of his own.

He had been hoping all his life to have a boat of his own, he said, and now finally he had enough money. For he wanted his craft to be good for anything, sardines, swordfish, tuna, rockcod, everything.

To be sure, the craft in time was built, all right, and was christened with Portuguese wine, and the celebration lasted all night, he was that happy.

Later, when the engines were installed and he was ready for the trial run, he had another celebration and invited us all aboard again. There must have been thirty of us on the little craft when we put out of the harbor. We were overcrowded and had to stand up most of the time, but we were not bored. Not to begin with, for Bachalachi would not permit us to be.

He was so excited over having a vessel of his own that he would not sit still. He kept racing over the deck and down into the engine room, coaxing as many of us as he could to go along with him. He had so many things he wanted to show us that he forgot, I guess, that his craft was little different from the other fishing crafts around here. Long before the end we all grew pretty tired of being dragged around, but he continued to go strong, and when his shirt became saturated with perspiration he took it off and continued racing around in his sleeveless undershirt.

"Come," he would say, thinking of a new place to take us, a place which was not new at all and which we already had seen. "Come." And he would start pulling us by the hand until finally we could stand it no longer and one of us said:

"My Good God, Bachalachi, we've seen the old tub, you know. Give us a rest."

This was not meant to be serious, for we all presumed we knew him too well for him to take us literally. But the excitement dissolved from his eyes and lips as though swabbed off by gasoline, and within a second another face had been put on his shoulders to replace the old happy one. And when we looked at him again he was not Bachalachi. He stared at us as though we deliberately had shot a fish-spear into him, then he limped back aft and sat down next the stern. He would not move. He would not talk. He would do nothing, only sit there, and this is the way he remained all the rest of the way back into port that evening.

The sweat dried on him and he should have put on his shirt or coat. He should not have sat there, as heated as he had been, without putting on something. We know this now because, hardy though we thought he was, his body apparently chilled into a cold, as pneumonia was what he died of that same week.

His bait-boat has been sold and re-sold since then. I do not know who is the present owner, but could find out by looking in the fishermen's register.

XXXIV

HE comes the nearest to being a hermit, I guess, of anybody around here. He is not old enough, though, to be a real hermit, and in addition he shaves. At least he was always shaven on the few times he came to town.

He did not select a very fanciful island for his hermitage either, if such is what it is. He lives on one of the two islands several miles to the south of here. The islands are sharp with a thorny brush, almost a mesquite. The sun hits the island on all sides at once. There is little shade for there are no trees. From a distance his island has the appearance of a burned biscuit which somebody has thrown away.

The cliffs are steep, and only by means of a tiny cove, called Pirate's Cove, may a decent landing be made at all. His hut is above the cove, and the Mexican Government pays him a few pesos a month to stay out there and tend a feeble beacon. But I think he would stay out there anyway.

Only about twice a year does he ever come to town. Sometimes he rows the twenty miles in his open lobster-boat, and sometimes if the

Mexican patrol boat happens to be passing he hoists a bit of bunting up the mast of his shack. The patrol boat puts into the cove, then, and brings him on into town.

His arrivals here usually make a feature story if the day is dull for other news. We take the usual picture and we write the usual line about what he does for entertainment. We write about his radio, about his books, and about how he stores up lobsters to sell on these trips to town. He traps the lobsters during the week or so in advance of his trip, and he stores them alive into a tiny lagoon within the cove. He keeps them trapped in there by sunken chicken-wire.

But what we do not write about is how he behaves after reaching town. He is everything but a hermit then, he is very much of the flesh. He comes to town primarily to buy coffee, shoes, socks, all such things as that to last him another year if need be. And when his purchases are completed he goes to Mrs. Morgan's where he is well known by her six girls. Or sometimes he goes directly there before he does his purchasing.

Mrs. Morgan's place is about five blocks from the water front and has a front yard with pepper trees and is surrounded by a hedge. Some of the neighbors have complained, but because the house is always so quiet and because it has a sign: Mrs. Morgan's Boarding House For Girls, the police do not interfere other than to visit her occasionally in a social way. She always greets the hermit as "El Hermito" just for the fun of it, although he can talk English as well as she can. In fact he is mostly English, although he can pass for a Mexican because of his sun-stricken skin.

For these islands have left their outdoor mark on him, all right. They apparently were once a part of a mainland peninsula, as the island on which he lives has rattlesnakes and tiny kangaroo mice. I doubt if they could have swum that far, twenty miles seeming quite a distance for a mouse to swim, and I have heard that rattlesnakes cannot swim any how. I have never seen any swimming, but again I do not know for sure.

These rattlers are rather small, and it seems as if an agreement has been reached between them and the sea gulls, cormorants and pelicans. For the birds occupy the other island almost exclusively. The rattlers take one island, the birds the other. The birds do all their nesting over there, and he prefers living with the rattlers instead of the birds, for the birds at times can become awfully noisy. They have run the government of their island for so long that they are drunk with their own power. They are more spoiled and more misbehaved than any of the birds which live around our port, and the hermit tells Mrs. Morgan that he is spoiled in the same way. He tells her that the reason he lives by himself is because he does not want to be bothered with anybody else.

"You'll get over that," she told him. "Something'll happen and you'll get over all that." And the funny part is that something did happen on the next trip or two.

We reporters had missed the hermit's arrival on the Mexican cutter, but hearing he was in town and because we were in need of a story the other morning reporter and I hunted him at Mrs. Morgan's. She is about fifty or fifty-five, dresses neatly, usually in gray, and tries never to embarrass us by having the girls around, although we probably would not mind. Her beer, though, is never green, and usually is the most excellent in town. She pours it slowly from the bottle to keep the yeast down on the bottom, and the last inch or two of the bottom she always throws away. A lot of people go there and, odd though it may seem, they sometimes take their wives after a dance.

But this was morning, and nobody else was in the front room except Mrs. Morgan and the hermit. He was a bit under, and not from beer. He apparently had been a bit under all night and now was preparing to leave to catch the patrol boat.

After greeting us and preparing our glasses she continued right on with her argument with the hermit. She was telling him about one of her girls named Katherine who was getting thinner and sicker all the time. "And not from what you may think either, El Hermito. For I have had her examined and have the certificate."

"T. B., then."

"No, not T. B. either, although it might soon well be."

"Then she's in the wrong business, that's all," he answered, and tried once more to make the outside door. But Mrs. Morgan shoved him back on the davenport.

"I know she's in the wrong business, you little fool. That's what I'm trying to tell you. Are you going to take her or aren't you?"

"I'm not. And anyway I don't run no health farm out there."

"You're going to start one, then," she said, motioning the other reporter and me to be patient.

"You're crazy," the hermit answered. "And she'd go crazy, too, inside three months. My food's the world's worst."

"Just the same she's going with you," Mrs. Morgan repeated. "I'm sending her to the boat now, and you're to take her and like it."

"The joke's on you, then. The skipper won't let women aboard."

"The joke's on you, then, because he will and he has. I've paid him, and Katherine's aboard right now. So you just run along."

"Well, I'll be—I'll be—" he tried to say to Mrs. Morgan, but failed.

This was more than a year ago. Yes, so much over a year ago that the other reporter and I were commenting about the conversation just the other day. We had not seen the hermit, nor for that matter had we seen a Mexican patrol boat recently. Our annual feature stories on the hermit would be ruined for all times if we hinted that he was not a hermit after all but was living with a girl. Yet thinking something may have happened to the both of them, a double-murder or a double-suicide or a double-starvation, and seeing the possibilities of a glorious story in the finding of their bodies on the isolated island, we talked to the pilot of the cruiser which runs outside to the fishing barge. We asked him if on his next trip he would take a roundabout route to the island and take us with him. This he did.

When our small cruiser put into Pirate's Cove the hermit himself greeted us and helped to make the line fast to a clump of brush. We delayed mentioning anything about the girl, fearing something might have happened to her and that he would be embarrassed. But he himself brought up the subject.

"I'm glad you came," he said. "It damn near looked like I'd have to make a trip to town myself."

"Why?"

"Oh, the kid's got something she wants sent to Mrs. Morgan. Here she comes now."

Sure enough. There she was, almost as copper as he was. She came hurrying down from the hut. She handed us a bunch of doilies embroidered out of what at one time must have been men's handkerchiefs, and she handed us eight rattlesnake rattles.

After her run she was trying to get her breath to speak, but the hermit spoke first: "That's her own embroidery, fellows. You ought to really look at it. And how you fixed on lobsters?"

So, for all I know this may be some sort of a love story. But I guess I had better wait three or four or five years more to make sure.

XXXV

WHEN we on the staff play poker we play with a two-bit limit, which is a pretty high limit for men receiving forty-five dollars a week. But we smoke cigars, we remove our coats, we forget the clock, and we pretend that forty-five dollars is not what we receive a week but a day.

We do not always play in the same place, but move from house to house. The married members of the staff invite us to their homes, and when the game becomes especially vicious it is a bit weird to realize that the host's wife and his youngsters are in another room keeping very quiet or sleeping. Or sometimes the wife goes to a picture show, as the rule of these games is for the wife not to show herself at all.

Because I have no dependents I usually try to break about even, or maybe lose a little, though not enough to hurt. So naturally Luck, which hates to be uncourted, showers her attention upon me and neglects the others. This is embarrassing, for the harder I try to put my winnings back into the pot the more interest they return me. And as sure as I start drawing the pot towards me I can hear a rustling of children in the bedroom, or imagine I can, and I do wish I never had started attending these poker sessions. Some night I may lose wretchedly and then may stop. But now, as long as I am ahead, I must go on and on.

The fellow-slaves pretend they do not care who wins, but not to care is hard when the wages of a day's work are lost on the table, when the man's efforts of the day have been cancelled and all he may do is report to work the next day to start over again.

In these games more than at our galley benches in the office we can watch each other growing older. We do not notice this month-by-month aging when our eyes are occupied with copy. But at night beneath the lights new lines show themselves eating gradually through the faces of my friends. The light brings out the thin spots in the hair, too, and once one of the older members appeared with his teeth out. They had been pulled earlier in the week, and because he could not sleep anyway he attended the game. He tried to be hilarious over what had happened to him, he joked about it as best he could through his raw gums. But I remember this man when he was little older than I am now. He too had stayed and stayed here, and now his teeth were gone, the first definite sign of the decadence which also was awaiting me.

There had been no advancement for him during these years, because on a small paper the advancement for anybody is infinitesimal. An office boy, if he is what managers call bright, advances to doing re-writes, then maybe to helping the police reporter, then maybe to being police reporter. That is, if he is what the managers call bright. But if he is real bright he usually sees in time the whole outlook and does not stay.

When my friend without the teeth came to the paper he came already an experienced man. His post then was the same as now, and fundamentally he was intelligent, too intelligent. No intelligent person like him should try to write editorials because the most popular editorials are always the obvious, and a real intelligent person does not deal with the obvious. That is why he was still with us that night playing poker. This was his reward for trying not to write the obvious. He was being out-drawn too. If he had three-of-a-kind I would have a straight. Or if he had a straight the former office boy, now courthouse reporter, would have a flush. This was the way it went all evening, the former office boy usually topping us all.

We all could see that the former office boy thought this life was great, this life of being with newspaper men. He, too, perhaps had seen the motion pictures of newspaper men supposedly in action. In pictures they drink and they play poker. He too could drink and now he was finding that he also could play poker. This newspaper life was just the thing, all right.

Another member of the staff arrived at the house late to enter the game. In the shift-about of chairs to make room, the former office boy moved to almost the identical place formerly occupied by my friend without the teeth.   The allegory in this shifting of places was so startling, so ridiculously startling, that I wanted to say something about it to somebody. I always have wanted to say something about it to somebody, but fortunately have refrained. For the fact that people grow old certainly is not front-page news, even when the change takes place like this one, all during the matter of a minute.

XXXVI

ANOTHER reason I no longer care to go around the world is because an around-the-world liner now comes here, once each year. The day is a busy one for us along the waterfront. We reporters meet the liner outside the channel at dawn, and in the evenings we ordinarily must hang around until the liner departs again, usually at midnight.

Yet for work the day is nothing compared to what it would be if I were packing for the trip myself, or if once aboard I were under the strain of trying to become acquainted with the interesting people of the adjoining cabin. I am most fortunate just to be able to stay here and let the interesting people come to me, if come they must.

In olden days I used to be sorry for these round-the-world passengers. They sailed with their life's savings expecting to find so much, but on reaching this port, the halfway point, they as yet had found nothing. I used to be sorry for them, but now I rather envy the constant hope which must be in them, a hope made the more eternal because so far they have not talked as intimately with Little Boy Blue as I have talked intimately with him.

This is his sixth trip around the world with these cruises. He is the publicity man as well as a sort of conductor. He tells the passengers what in each city they should see and what in each city they would do well to buy as mementos. We reporters have called him Little Boy Blue from the very start, the name being one he brought with him. The agonies of each voyage he unburdens on us, realizing we never would be buying round-the-world tickets anyhow.

He has typewritten stories about the more celebrated passengers aboard. To save us time in meeting our editions he hands us these stories, or if we like he will usher the celebrated passengers before us in the music-room to be passed on by the judgment of our own tribunal. But after the first rush work is completed and after our editions have been met, we relax over our Bacardi and our talk-talk, and we hear him say: "Guess what I toldem to buy in your burg this trip?"

We cannot guess, of course, because he has some of his ports famous for their canes, others for their crockery, others for their shawls, and he does not always stick to the same item the next trip around. Our own port, for instance, he has had famous respectively for its Navajo

rugs, its pine-knot wood carvings, and its miniature warships for children. But this time when
he asked us and we could not answer him, he
said: "I told'em cactus plants. And for godsakes
you got any? I thought I saw some here the
other trip."

We assured him he was comparatively safe.
And sure enough. For later that night, when I
was up in my studio on the topside of the tugboat pier, I watched the passengers returning to
their vessel. I could look down on them as they
stepped from their taxicabs or as they came
walking from uptown. There they were, from
their day ashore, with their cameras and their
canes and their overcoats, for they will take
their overcoats ashore no matter how lukewarm
the weather, and among their day's purchases
were the telltale shoe-boxes in which the florists
around here pack their tiny cacti plants for
customers.

Nights down here on the waterfront are not
at all like daytimes. It is as if while we are away
to supper somebody comes along and redecorates
the whole shoreline. The lights along the
embarcadero multiply in the water, and when a
shoreboat noses along cutting the surface the
lights multiply still more. So strange is the
change here between nighttimes and daytimes
that for all I know I too could have moved to

Constantinople, and I could have moved there without the bother of lugging along my body, my overcoat, my suitcases, my cacti plants, and I am always glad when the round-the-world liner finally pulls out of port again, the plight of the occupants somehow having filled me with the same depression as watching shackled prisoners being transported.   And of course Little Boy Blue also is to blame.   He has been so honest with us.   Without really knowing what he was doing he has impressed on me how many times I, too, have gone around and around and around the world while sitting with my cigarettes in this tiny tugboat room of mine.

For if I really must see a change I always may look aloft and watch the unfolding of the latest transfiguration of the clouds, the night clouds specially.   And if I must feel aloof, immeasurably aloof from the moneyed travellers, I merely need imagine that Little Boy Blue, in a moment of humor, has seriously said to them in the evening:

"This is the town where Max Miller lives. You know, Max Miller, the waterfront reporter. That is his room up there, the room with the yellow light in it. Yes, to be sure, you've all heard of him, you've all heard of that waterfront reporter who never goes away."

XXXVII

ONE summer on my vacation I decided to go home, the first time after coming here. I resolved not to be melancholy on arriving. I would pretend to myself I had not dedicated all these years to marking time in one place. I would secretly hypnotize myself into the illusion I was everything the home folks had predicted for me, and the campus had predicted for me, and my old editor on the town's paper had predicted for me.

To aid the illusion I would smoke cigars, and I would maintain an aura of wise silence. I would pose as one given to listening, not talking. Each day of my visit I would wear my best suit, the one of blue broadcloth.

To reach my home town it is first necessary to take a steamship to Seattle. Six days. The line offered me the trip for all the stories I had given it throughout the years. To get by the Interstate Commerce rules prohibiting passes to non-employees, the captain listed me as a cook's helper. But I slept on an extra bunk in his quarters, and I ate with him, and I could have used my trip to the south or to the west, but I

went north.   I would put an end to this dread of
returning home.   The dread had turned into a
complex.

Perhaps I should have let the dread remain a
complex.   Perhaps I should not have tried to get
rid of it.   I don't know.   But I do know that I
who would have been writing with the immortals
was coming home.   There must be thousands of
us.   Each train must be carrying home at least
one of us.   Each vessel too, must have at least
one of us aboard.   We are sick, we are ill, we are
diseased.   We have no message to give because
we are too burned with our ambition to give
messages.   In our hungry desperation to see
more than others see we over-focus our field
glasses, and instead of creating a second-sight
we create a blur.   We are suicidal, blind; we are
clever, but not clever enough.   We are wise, but
our wisdom is without direction.   We lug it
around only to annoy us.

I lugged mine to the picket gate of my home.
Our house was the only one on the street which
still retained its pickets.   They were first put
there to protect the cherry trees and the pear
trees.   And they were put there, too, out of
habit.   All houses had fences, it seems, when our
house was built.   I can recall the boldness of the
first neighbors who dared to remove this protection.   We youngsters must have been considered

a bad crop. Yet there was our fence still standing with the stubbornness of a religion. The
pickets were sermons to keep out sin. The gate
was weighed open and shut by a lard-bucket of
stones. This was my home, then, the same as it
had been ten years ago, twenty years ago. There
used to be ten of us living in that house. And
now only my mother and father retained the
guard. They were Methodists.

They were inside the house now. I knew this,
although I could not see them or hear them. Nor
was smoke lifting from the chimney. But I knew
they were there because a small washing hung
on the clothes-reel. The same clothes-reel. It
spun around so Mother could hang the clothes
while standing on one spot. Mother never left
the yard when clothes were hanging outside to
dry. She was afraid of rain or of sudden wind.
She was afraid some shirt might be whipped off
the wires and torn. The clothes-reel had been a
sensation long ago when father had first obtained
it for her. The clothes-reel had been a luxury.

The pear trees in the yard had gone without
pruning. The stubby branches reached out
wherever they pleased. They were like her
departed family. I was the youngest. We had
been caught hard in the Renaissance striking
our generation. My oldest brother alone continued to believe in a God with a beard. Heaven

had awarded his faith by making him rich. He sent a check home each month larger than I could send in a year. He was good. His Hereafter was assured him. He is the one in the family who cautiously owned "Perfect Manhood." He had bought the book from an evangelist. The evangelist had given a lecture in the Y. M. C. A., then had sold the books. It had a black cover and it advised men how to be physically strong. Strength could be obtained only by celibacy. He had told me that if I was to be a strong football player on the high school team I must never have a vile thought. I was not then in high school, I was still in the fourth or fifth grade, but I remember how hard I worked trying not to have a vile thought. I would think I had gone along all morning without having a vile thought, and then one would come to me. Vile thoughts, the evangelist said, frequently resulted in the face becoming pimpled. After each vile thought I would anxiously feel my cheeks and my throat. I would sometimes go to the mirror in the bathroom. I would climb onto a chair and look, for the mirror was adjusted for the brothers to shave with. I wondered how long it would take for the pimple to come. I searched the book but it did not tell me, and I was afraid to ask my brother. He would know then that I was doomed to grow up without muscles in my arms.

To try to arrange one's memories with their respective ages is most difficult. I learned this for a certainty as I moved along the picket fence towards the gate. Ages came just any old time, and so did incidents. That pear tree, for example. The pear tree nearest the clothes-reel. This was the tree on which my sister and I played Angel. I surely was not old enough to be in school at that time, and yet the picture was as clear as "Perfect Manhood." From newspapers she and I cut long wide strips. These were wings. We would pin them to our shoulders with safety pins, then leap from the tree to the ground.

I wonder how often we played this game. Not many times, surely. Yet it seems as if we had played it an entire summer, so distinct is the recollection. But my practical mind knows better. We surely only played it three or four times because of quarrels. She began slicing the edges of her wings with scissored fringes for feathers. She could do this, she said, because she was a lady angel. But being a man angel I must retain simple wings. For me to have fringes was not playing fair. The ban was lifted only on that Sunday afternoon when she conceived the idea of cutting her wings from the brilliant page of the colored comic section.

On that day I was permitted fringes on my wings, but not colors. Yet the decree did me no good. I was about to make my first flight from heaven to earth with my fringed wings when my father came into the yard. He had heard us quarreling, and he reminded us that the day was the Sabbath and that angels must not fly around on the Sabbath. We unpinned our wings and never felt like playing Angel again. Perhaps we merely grew older a bit overnight without actually knowing what had happened to us.

As I walked along the picket fence I had a memory for each picket. But the memories were not distinct like pickets. Rather, the memories were all bunched together in a solid lump. Nor could I select which memory I wanted; they came to me of their own choosing. Yet if I stayed outside the fence long enough I could have all of them. That is, I could have all I wanted. The disagreeable memories, the ones I did not desire to see again, I could turn back into hiding the instant they touched me. I could ward them off. I was wearing an armor. I presume everybody returning home wears an armor.

I placed my hand on the gate. It opened too easily. It opened almost of its own accord. It should not have opened so easily. I was not quite ready yet. More stones should have been in the lard bucket. I looked, but no stones were in it at all. The bottom had rusted away.

Everything then, the gate, the bucket and the stones had plotted for my quick entrance. Before I was prepared, I found myself standing inside the gate. I was as an actor shoved out upon the stage before his cue. I did not know my lines.

The play for which I had been rehearsing these past many years was a different one, written by a different author. In that play I was to have arrived home in a custom-built car, a car which I was to present to my parents. My mother and father were to have been on the front porch waiting for me. They had heard of my coming by reading the newspapers. I was to have reckoned on this, yet have pretended my arrival was a surprise. I would have said, "Well, Mother, here's your kid. Back again." The neighbors would have laughed at this. For in the background of my plans there were to have been neighbors. They would have been standing around outside on the street. They too would have been tipped off on my coming. I would have escorted my mother back into the house, my father following, and all would have been as it should be.

I would have said, "Remember, Dad, when you kicked me out of that pear tree one Sunday?" I would have said this later, of course, much later, hours later, as we sat reminiscently by the

sitting-room window looking out over the old
lawn.

He would have answered, "I sure do, Son. I
sure do. The blame thing hasn't yielded a pear
since."

I would have said, "Dad, how would you and
Mother like to move into a new house of stucco?
One without an awful upstairs to climb, and on
the other side of town? On the Bayside? Well,
I have such a house ready for you. Come, we'll
take a ride before dinner and look at it."

He would have answered, "Now, now, my boy,
this house has served us thirty years. Be careful. Still, if a new place would be easier on
your mother. . . ."

But the play of my illusion was over. And I
found myself out upon the stage in a different
costume. The click of the gate behind me announced the rising of the curtain. It was now
up to me to walk around the house to the back
door. Should I knock? Or should I walk right
in? Would I frighten them if I walked right in?

And all the while I was debating this, I was
moving. My feet were taking me around the
side of the house; I was following the boardwalk, the same, patched boardwalk.

For even waterfront reporters occasionally return home.

XXXVIII

WHAT! Is this all? Where are all the thousands of notes I had in secret storage for this book? Where are all the thoughts I have brooded on so long? Where are those dozens of maxims I was to give to the country? And the epigrams? And the stanzas of advice?

I know. They are outside the window there. I can see them hovering over the bay. They see me too, but they will not come to me. They prefer their winged freedom to being captured and placed on paper. They prefer grinning at me, giggling at my attempts to be a book-writer. "Get back to your job, reporter. Get back to collecting names, names, names." Ho, they have overheard the instructions all right, they know I am the waterfront reporter, nothing more. Why should they obey when I beg them to come back? These thoughts which are mine and yet not mine?

They know only too well that while the world whizzes around me, while men are made and unmade, while science is in its renaissance, they know only too well that through all this scramble I am content to stay here in this sunny port getting names, names, names. I am a nothing—a nothing with lungs to keep me a mortal and with eyes for recording names.

And they know too that I have written as much of a book as I can write. And they know too that the pieces refuse to stitch themselves together into a plot, into a novel with hero and heroine, into a theme, into a purpose. I lose: they win—do the thoughts outside the window there, thoughts which belong to me but will not remain with me because they like their freedom better.

The End.